Shared
beliefs

Different
lives

Shared beliefs
Different lives

Women's Identities
in Evangelical Context

Lori G. Beaman

Chalice Press.
St. Louis, Missouri

Bible quotations, unless otherwise noted, are from the *New Revised Standard Version Bible,* copyright 1989, Division of Christian Education of the National Council of the Churches of Christ in the United States of America. Used by permission. All rights reserved.

Cover design: Wendy Barnes
Art director: Elizabeth Wright
Interior design: Wynn Younker

This book is printed on acid-free, recycled paper.

Visit Chalice Press on the World Wide Web at
www.chalicepress.com

10 9 8 7 6 5 4 3 2 1   99 00 01 02 03

Library of Congress Cataloging–in–Publication Data

Beaman, Lori G.
   Shared beliefs, different lives : women's identities in Evangelical context /
by Lori G. Beaman.
      p.   cm.
   Includes bibliographical references and index.
   ISBN 0-8272-3444-9
   1. Protestant women   2. Evangelicals.   3. Protestant women—Atlantic
Provinces—Interviews.   4. Evangelicals—Atlantic Provinces—Interviews.
I. Title.
   BR1640 .B43   1999   99–050431
   280'.4'0820971—dc21   C1P

Printed in the United States of America

For my grandmothers,
Nada Price and Gertrude Beaman

Contents

Preface

During the process of writing this book there were many people who contributed in a variety of ways. I owe a great debt of gratitude to the women who participated in this research. They gave generously of their time and freely shared intimate aspects of their lives with me. I have tried to present their experiences in a manner that honors their worldview.

I would like to thank Nancy Nason-Clark for her gentle but persistent inquiries about the progress of the book and her unwavering support and encouragement to continue writing over a period of three years. I am also grateful to Jon Berquist, the editor with whom I have worked at Chalice Press, who has been faithful in his interest and encouragement throughout the project. Thanks are also owed to Shannon Roset and Kristine Peace, who were meticulous and dependable research assistants.

Thank you also to each of my friends who has helped me to heal over the past two years. I would not have had the energy to finish this project without your support.

This research was supported financially by the Social Science and Humanities Research Council of Canada, as well as the Religion and Violence Research Team at the Muriel McQueen Fergusson Centre for Family Violence Research at the University of New Brunswick.

Introduction

As I began to study evangelical women, I became increasingly intrigued with how they construct their world, balancing Christian commitment with secular ideologies and pressures. I was especially interested in how they negotiate their way through everyday life. I often heard women talk about this process as being "in the world but not of it." In part, this research was about exploring what exactly that means. How, I wondered, do conservative Protestant women use their Christian commitment as a map to guide them through the complexities of modern life? To what extent does the Christian worldview act as a prescriptive guide to life? How is it used as an explanatory key to everyday events?

Like some of you who read this book, I came to this project as an outsider. Although I have some religious background with evangelical Christianity as a child, I certainly do not fit into the definition of "Christian" as it is understood by evangelical Christians. I do not attend church on a regular basis, my network of friends is not composed of churched individuals, although it certainly includes those for whom organized religion is important, and my call to service is not rooted in a desire to witness for Jesus Christ. As an outsider I have tried to learn the language of this community of believers, in addition to being able to recognize their material culture and to distinguish the necessary from the optional in their faith-related practices. In particular I am interested in how women make sense of their Christian commitment as a map to guide their relations with their husbands and children, their faith communities, and the world beyond. To what extent do evangelical women live under a sacred canopy of meaning? How do they interpret patriarchal dogma in the course of everyday living?

My work with the Religion and Violence Research Team at the Muriel McQueen Fergusson Center for Family Violence Research in eastern Canada opened the door to the evangelical community. Most of the team members are themselves evangelicals, and it was my association with them and the team that facilitated my entry into evangelical culture. Prior to conducting the ninety-four in-depth interviews that form the basis of the discussion in this book, I was involved in a team project that involved the collection of data through questionnaires and interviews with evangelical clergy. The team also conducted thirty focus groups with church women, which was my initial point of contact with the women whose stories are told in the following pages. It was through these experiences that I began to be able to speak the language and to recognize the unique elements of evangelical culture, which allowed me to negotiate my way through the world of evangelical women.

The women I interviewed graciously shared their ideas and beliefs with me, allowing me to understand how they translate their beliefs into practice on a day-to-day basis. They shared intimate thoughts with me in the process of helping me to make sense of what it means in day-to-day terms to call oneself an evangelical Christian. Their love of God was unfaltering. They were sometimes critical of clergy and church hierarchies. More often, however, they focused on their shared experiences with other church women, whether as wives, as mothers, or in their roles as service providers to their faith communities.

Although evangelical women are unique, they also have much in common with women who do not share their worldview. The quiet revolution that has seen the entry of large numbers of women into the paid labor force has posed unique challenges and raised complex questions for all women. Women who participate in the paid labor force struggle to balance work and family. Women who stay at home to be with their children are often made to feel as though they are missing out or are somehow inadequate. Social pressures are such that either route is fraught with guilt and self-doubt. Reproductive issues, such as birth control and abortion, also pose special dilemmas for women. All women, regardless of their faith commitments, have in common the social pressures surrounding gender roles, which have become so prevalent in the latter part of this century. How women respond to these pressures is mediated by their specific life histories, including race, religion, and socioeconomic status.

Evangelical women struggle with the daily negotiation of values and actions, asking themselves how to be good wives, mothers, and citizens. They attempt to preserve a sense of self and agency in a culture that demands much self-sacrifice, within a faith community that reinforces the message of self-sacrifice as a model of Christian living. Evangelical women suffer guilt over participation in the paid labor force, often, like their secular counterparts, working a double day, first in their paid jobs and then at home. We might argue that they work a third shift through service to their faith communities. As for other women, juggling these multiple roles sometimes leads to burnout. Similar to their secular sisters, evangelical women prioritize their mothering role and struggle to find ways to fulfill that role as well as they can.

As a feminist, I confess that the world of evangelical women sometimes poses some interesting challenges for me. I cannot fathom why a woman would want to call her husband her "head," even though she may live in a partnership with him. I am also troubled by the homophobic stance of many of the evangelicals I have interviewed. I wonder about the economic roots of women's complicity with patriarchal dogma. I worry that the pressure to be perfect is too much for some women as they juggle family, church, and participation in the paid labor force. Perhaps more than any other group of women, Christian women are supposed to be able to "do it all"—to be good mothers, tireless church citizens, and worthy examples of the power and love of the Lord to the secular community.

Throughout the fieldwork, analysis, and writing of this book I have tried to be true to the words of the women I interviewed. Although I do not share their worldview, I respect the fact that for these women their faith is a way to find meaning in the world. I began the research with a commitment to explore beyond the surface of doctrines that have been so problematic for outsiders, and especially for feminists. I started with the assumption that even in the face of patriarchy, women exercise agency in ways that maximize their own potential.

I also wanted to leave space for the recognition that women bring a variety of identities to their daily lives—evangelical, mother, victim of abuse, feminist professional, and so on. While these identities are often brought together as a coherent whole, they sometimes cause disjunctures that affect how women interpret and act on events that occur in day-to-day life. A multi-layered analysis is an important beginning place to explore the ways women bring together multiple identities. From here, it is possible to identify patterns of the ways in which women interpret events and negotiate within their families, their churches, and their social contexts.

A major theme that emerged from the data is diversity. Even as I write "evangelical women," I cringe at the limitations of this category. In an attempt to broaden the boundaries of such rigid categorization, I develop a typology (which is also reflected in other research on church women) that identifies three major streams of ideological approach among the whole group of women who participated in this research. Traditionalists object to women's participation in the paid labor force, interpret biblical passages more literally, and adhere to a traditional division of labor between men and women. In sharp contrast, feminist evangelicals reject the rhetoric of submission and call for an articulation of male-female relations as partnerships. They embrace women's equality and call for increased roles for women within church hierarchies. Moderates accept biblical teachings on submission and headship but live and interpret them as partnership and equality within their own marital relationships. They accept liberal feminist notions of equality quite readily but are cautious about extremism in any form. This latter group makes up the greatest proportion of the women whose voices are heard in this book.

From an academic standpoint, this study gives us a window into the world of evangelical women. It offers challenges to analyses that portray this group of women as monolithic, and it questions the characterization of conservative Protestant women as anti-feminist. Although conservative Protestant women are often perceived as "submissive servants" or "doormats" by those who do not espouse an evangelical worldview, this book offers an alternative vision of evangelical women as purposeful agents who negotiate the boundaries of their faith in the process of day-to-day living. The book explores the diversity, as well as the similarities, among women who describe themselves as evangelical Christians. The data is presented so that church women speak for themselves on their faith commitments, their marriages, their roles, feminism, and violence against women. In general, this book seeks to answer the question, What does it mean to be an evangelical woman?

For those who come to this discussion as evangelical Christians, I hope that the voices of the women resonate with your own experiences. This book gives insight into the unique challenges faced by evangelical women today. The stresses and pressure for perfection are great, and they often exist with inadequate support from the church, which continues to make extraordinary demands on its female members. Although women are often able to draw on the resources provided by church women's groups and their sisters in faith, church leaders need to examine the inequity of the demands placed on the women in their congregations.

I do not claim that this book has the answers to all of the issues raised above, but it does give us insight into evangelical life from the standpoint of women. Although there is an increasing amount of information about church groups, we still need to understand the unique role of these groups for women. How do they reflect individual religiosity? What is the nature of the service commitment of church women during the course of their lives? What impact does that service have on the faith and secular communities? In the following pages we hear the voices of evangelical women as they describe the importance of their faith and the ways in which it impacts on their relationships with family, church, and community.

1

Understanding Women's Faith and Agency

*My Christian beliefs make a **huge** difference in my life—in everything that I do and in the peace that I have and in the strength that I have. That is sort of the starting ground of everything that I do, you know, you start the day saying, God help me to be more patient, help me to be kind to everybody I meet, you know. Sorry for what I did yesterday, help me to try better today. Really, it is a huge grounding in my day-to-day life.*

In today's society, which has been characterized as a smorgasbord of religious ideas and choices, what does it mean to live within a framework that shapes one's day from beginning to end? Evangelical women interpret the demands of family, church, and society in ways that they see as being consistent with a religious worldview that prescribes their relationships with their husbands, their church, and their self-presentation in society. They model submission, service to others, and a witness of their personal relationships with Jesus in each of these contexts. Within the rhetoric of evangelicalism, there would seem to be little room for choice and a limited possibility for variation among women. Yet such a picture of religious practice would fail to account for individual religious actors and the ways in which they interpret the world around them.

Although there has been a flurry of academic research around the topic of evangelical Christianity in the past decade, there remains a paucity of information about the ways in which the evangelical worldview is translated in the daily lives of conservative Protestant women. Using data collected through in-depth interviews with ninety-four evangelical women over a two-year period, this book explores the ways in which evangelical women interpret, react to, shape, and incorporate church teachings in their everyday lives. Conservative Protestant women are sometimes perceived as "submissive servants" or "doormats" by those who do not espouse an evangelical worldview, a view that this book seeks to challenge. This book offers an alternative vision, through women's stories, of evangelical women as purposeful agents who negotiate the boundaries of their faith in the process of day-to-day living.

Deconstructing simplistic conceptualizations of evangelical women involves challenging two assumptions: first, that patriarchal dogma can be taken at face value, and second, that women who choose to espouse a worldview and social context that is patriarchal can be dismissed as "doormats" or as possessing a "false consciousness." Rather, the ways in which women act as agents in their interpretation of teachings such as submission and headship, and more generally about women's roles, need to be closely examined, beginning with their own lived experiences. Further, a contextualized and nuanced approach to agency recognizes that dualistic conceptualizations of women's agency miss the shades of gray that are a part of the daily negotiation of life. Women are not simply victims or agents, but are constantly interpreting and shaping structure in the course of their day-to-day living as evangelical Christians.

The Evangelical Worldview

Evangelical Christians see the world as moving away from Christ, and thus it is their task to both preserve existing Christian "territory" and to increase its boundaries. Their beliefs provide them with both hope and guidance on this front, and in the course of their everyday lives as they work through their marriages, raising children, and dealing with the world. The church provides a constant affirmation of beliefs and a space in which evangelicals can come together with like-minded individuals. However, for evangelicals, religion and daily life are not separable. In their relationships with their husbands, children, fellow Christians, and the secular world, evangelical women bring to bear their beliefs about how to live a Christian life as prescribed by God's word. I often heard women exclaim that they did not know how people got through life without the help and support of God. Their worldview is both a prescriptive and an explanatory model for living in society. It is prescriptive in the sense that it guides their lives through notions of what and how a Christian should be in daily life, and explanatory because everyday events are interpreted through the lense of evangelicalism, including the belief that life's blessings and disappointments are explainable as the "will of God." The idea of a worldview is not used here as a static concept; rather, inherent in the notion of worldview as it is used in the following chapters is the notion of process and change. The construction of a religious worldview is an ongoing, dialectical process that involves both the individual and social processes (Berger, 1969:45). For example, while women's roles have been centered around the "divinized home," which invests the home with sacred meaning and sees women as the religious agent and moral guardian (DeBerg, 1990:148), evangelical women are now present in the workplace in the same percentage as their secular counterparts. This has resulted in *some* accommodation for working women within evangelical culture, although there is diverse opinion among evangelicals about working mothers. To speak, therefore, of "the" evangelical worldview is somewhat misleading; evangelicals are diverse, sometimes so much so that their differences result in schism (Ammerman, 1990; Warner, 1988). We can, however, attempt to identify some common beliefs and practices among those who identify themselves as evangelicals.

Evangelicalism is described by Hunter as "theologically conservative Protestantism," which includes fundamentalism (1987b:3).[1] Often confused at the popular level with fundamentalism, evangelicals do share with fundamentalists a belief in biblical inerrancy and spiritual salvation as being possible only through a personal relationship with Jesus Christ. One way to

---

[1]One important issue emerging from the study of evangelicals that is taken up by scholars like Hunter (1987b) and Shibley (1996) is the extent to which evangelicalism has affected American culture.

conceptualize evangelicalism is on a theological continuum, ranging from fundamentalism with its clear, nonnegotiable boundaries, to a liberal position in which boundaries are more blurred and where there is a greater accommodation to the secular world. Evangelicalism is not easily defined, due in part to its diversity (Marsden, 1987; Rothenberg, 1987)[2] and to confusion over its status as a set of beliefs, a community, or a movement (Marsden, 1987). The literature does, however, reveal some tenets that are generally presented as being central to the evangelical worldview from which a beginning model or "ideal type" can be constructed.

Essential to evangelicalism is a set of theological tenets that form the basis of evangelical beliefs. These include: (a) the Bible as the "final authority in matters of faith and practice" (Hunter, 1987a; see also Marsden, 1987:59); (b) the "deity and historicity of Jesus Christ" (Hunter, 1987a:51); (c) salvation only through a personal relationship with and trust in Jesus Christ (Hunter, 1987a:51; Marsden, 1987:59), often achieved through a crisis conversion (Nock, 1993:53)[3], and (d) the importance of evangelism, that is, spreading the message of salvation (Marsden, 1987:59; Hunter, 1987a:51). Doctrines surrounding family life include the undesirability of divorce and biblically prescribed family relations (Rose, 1993; Ammerman, 1987). John Stackhouse associates evangelical life with "doctrinal orthodoxy, personal piety, and evangelism" (1993:181). A significant daily challenge for evangelicals is to live "in the world, but not of it," meaning that while it is important for them to make their presence felt in secular culture, and in fact to transform secular culture by "leading people to Christ," it is important that their culture not become con-taminated by worldly ways. The nature and strength of evangelical boundaries between secular culture and their own world vary over time and place.

How and to what extent these tenets are incorporated in the everyday lives of evangelicals is not always clear. In other words, there is sometimes a disjuncture between ideology and practice. For example, despite the emphasis placed on evangelism, Nancy

---

[2]The heterogeneous nature of evangelicalism is well illustrated in Steve Warner's study of a changing religious community (1988).

[3]Shibley describes the born-again experience as "a spiritual rebirth, acknowledging personal sinfulness and Christ's atonement" (1996:20).

Ammerman (1987) found that many of the Bible believers in her study were reluctant to proselytize and were indeed uncomfortable with that role. While they expressed belief in the importance of evangelism, the participants in Ammerman's study did not often translate the belief into practice, at least in the narrower conceptualization of evangelizing, such as door-to-door proselytizing or other such approaches with strangers to share the word of God. Reginald Bibby has made a similar finding in Canada (1995). As we will see, the evangelical women I talked to translate the call to evangelize in the broad sense of modeling a Christian life to others, not as a need to go calling door-to-door.

The translation of belief into practice is further complicated when beliefs are not shared among all evangelicals, as is the case with certain social justice issues. The place of a social gospel, that is, the evidencing of a Christian commitment to benefit society through good works, and its prominence in evangelical life continue to be controversial. One of the most confusing aspects of evangelical political action is the extent to which it is associated with the Christian Right and the New Right. Some of the more publicized issues that have engaged the Christian Right include abortion, prayer in schools, and anti-gay and -lesbian campaigns (Wilcox, 1994). While evangelicals share some of these concerns, research suggests that the relationship between adhering to an evangelical worldview and activism on any particular issue is complex (Hunter, 1987b; Rhodes, 1985). In particular, many evangelical Christians are leery of any activity that would allow them to be pegged as extremists.

Although evangelical and New Right agendas sometimes coalesce, it is important to see these as two distinct groups. As Rebecca Klatch has argued, there are at least two streams of New Right conservatism, one of which is rooted in laissez-faire approaches to government and economics and is not related to religious ideology at all (1987). While the other stream emerges from conservative Protestantism, not all evangelicals can be pegged as supporters of the New Right agenda. In fact, as Klatch argues, there is frequent disagreement between these two New Right streams of ideology. Of the three aspects of New Right ideology—economic libertarianism, social traditionalism, and militant anticommunism—it is the second in which evangelical Christians are most interested. Peggy Shriver points out that support for the political conservatism of the New Right among evangelical Christians is actually quite limited (1989). Again, for the majority of evangelical women, any form of extremism is to be eschewed, be it the political agenda of the New Right or radical feminism.[4]

Although social justice continues to be an ongoing source of debate among evangelicals, Hunter suggests that there is emerging support for social ministry as an end in itself (1987b:43; see Bibby, 1995). However, as Hunter's research suggests, evangelicals are less likely to compromise on issues relating to family breakdown and the role of women, and therefore "individuals, organizations, political movements and social trends oriented away from this model (such as feminism and homosexuality) would be viewed as threatening" (1987b:82).[5] The extent to which evangelical women incorporate secular ideologies such as feminism is one of the questions explored in this book. To what extent do biblical teachings, such as "There is no longer male and female,"[6] overlap with feminist notions of equality?

Together with the ideological tenets of evangelicalism discussed above, there is a distinctive evangelical material culture. Wheeler (1996) has identified a pervasive culture of evangelical Christians that does not necessarily have ideological under-pinnings. Wheeler maps a distinctive material culture of conservative Protestant Christians, which ranges from "Bible cozies" (hand-knit or -sewn covers) to pamphlets. She argues that this material culture is an important aspect of evangelical Christian identity—it is part of how they know who they are, and it distinguishes them from other religiously motivated groups. It is evangelical women who are primarily responsible for the creation

----

[4]For a more detailed discussion, see Beaman, 1997.

[5]Individualist theology is manifested in the tendency for evangelicals to individuate personal, social, and institutional problems. In other words, problems are caused by the sinful hearts and minds of humans (Hunter, 1987b:51). Ted Jelen's study of clergy as political leaders points to a further complication: An emphasis on individualist theology among evangelicals may preclude or limit clergy leadership on this issue. "Political issues such as defense or economic assistance to the disadvantaged seem tangential to the primary task of facilitating individual conversions" (1994:30), at least among the clergy Jelen interviewed. According to Hunter, the individualist tendency is also mirrored in the attitudes and practices of lay members of evangelical churches (1987a).

[6]Galatians 3:28.

and maintenance of this "Bible cozy" culture, through crafts and the careful creation of a welcoming home atmosphere.

Is there an evangelical worldview? As we shall see, for women, it involves an ethic of service, emphasis on their mothering/ nurturing role, a belief that they are different from secular culture and that it is desirable to be different. It means reading Christian books, associating with Christian friends and engaging in Christian activities. A daily relationship with God, strengthened through prayer and devotions, is central. It also, for women, incorporates frequent contact with other Christian women through Bible study groups, mission and prayer groups, and other social gatherings. There is an evangelical worldview whose ideological tenets are mediated by women in their daily lives as mothers, wives, homemakers, and workers in the paid labor force. Not only is the evangelical worldview molded from within, it is also vulnerable to secular forces and influences.

Agency in a Patriarchal Context

Central to the exploration of evangelical life is the broader issue of agency and structure: How do evangelical women exercise agency in the context of a patriarchal religious structure? How do they understand their own action in the context of their families, church structure, and social life? Gerda Lerner describes patriarchy as

> the manifestation and institutionalization of male dominance over women and children in the family and the extension of male dominance over women in society in general. It implies that men hold power in all the important institutions of society and that women are deprived of access to such power. It does *not* imply that women are either totally powerless or totally deprived of rights, influence, and resources. (1986:239)

Religious culture has charged women with the existence of sin, citing Eve as its origin. Women have been excluded, or marginalized, from powerful leadership positions, while being charged with responsibility for endless mundane tasks involved in the operation of churches. Many women have entrusted clergy with their children, only to discover that they have suffered abuse at the hands of church leaders (Nason-Clark, 1993).

An important task in examining patriarchy in the context of religious organizations is to deconstruct its multiple layers, as well as to avoid a bifurcated or polarized categorization of women as either having or not having power. Thus, we need to think about power not in episodic terms, or as one person imposing her will on another (Clegg, 1993:28), but as a relational construct that is located in agents' interactions. Power then becomes a "process that may pass through distinct circuits of power and resistance" (1993:28). This concept of power encompasses both the enabling and constraining aspects of power, as well as its prohibitive and productive nature. The relational nature of power is illustrated through women's interactions with each other and with the church organization. Seeing men as having all of the power and exercising it over women is too simplistic. A relational conceptualization of power allows us to develop a multilayered notion of the agency-structure dynamic that is not reduced to men telling women what to do. This is not to deny the patriarchal nature of religious institutions, but to encourage a thorough explication of the process of power relations.

One of the tasks taken up by feminist research is to delineate the parameters of patriarchy. However, a simultaneous objective is to reveal the multiple forms of women's agency in the context of a culture that facilitates women's oppression in a myriad of ways. This is not always an easy task: While we want to celebrate women's agency, we must also be cautious about obscuring systemic disadvantages that persist even in the face of individual and group agency. Moreover, the degree to which women see themselves as being disadvantaged by being excluded from pastoral or financial authority also varies. The temptation to lapse into false consciousness discussions becomes almost over-whelming when one hears evangelical women claim that they have no interest in being in positions that have traditionally been held by men. Yet the ways in which women *do* exercise power have remained relatively unexplored. Church women's groups, for example, provide a forum in which women empower each other and occasionally mobilize for political action on issues that are often associated with feminist "causes," such as violence against women. Teasing out the rhetoric and the practice becomes a central process in understanding evangelical women's agency.

Evangelical women are not alone in their acceptance of religious dogma that, at least at face value, is stiflingly patriarchal.

Nancy Ammerman has explored the everyday experiences of submission and headship dilemmas among fundamentalists (1987); Lynn Davidman (1986) and Debra Kaufman (1991) have examined the attraction of Jewish Orthodoxy to some women; Mary Jo Neitz (1987) has assessed women's explanations of and reactions to conservative doctrines in relation to gender roles within the Catholic charismatic movement; Susan Palmer (1995) has reviewed women's experiences in new religious movements; and Olshan and Schmidt (1994) have examined the doctrinally prescribed subordinate status of Amish women.

In her book *Rachel's Daughters: Newly Orthodox Jewish Women*, Debra Kaufman explores and maps women's agency within Orthodox Judaism. Through the eyes of the women she interviews, Kaufman sees that, rather than being oppressive, the separation of women's roles and their physical segregation provide a source of empowerment. However, Kaufman does go on to argue that women's culture does not necessarily develop from such separation. She argues that "it may do nothing more than limit women to their own sphere of activities, networks, and rituals, thereby reinforcing the status quo" (1991:129). Kaufman's work illustrates the complexities of women's agency in the context of a patriarchal religious structure. On the surface, the maintenance of women-only spaces resembles a radical feminist separatist ideal. The difference, though, is that Orthodox Jewish women do not challenge male hegemony (1991:160), nor does their approach to gender roles "directly address the politics of religious patriarchy or the division of labor that helps to maintain it" (1991:161). Thus, although women are active agents in patriarchal religious settings, their agency may not be politically motivated, nor does it always challenge the patriarchal structure of religion.

What many of the researchers who explore conservative religions and women have in common is their commitment to the explication of patriarchal doctrine from the perspective of the women who experience their religion as primary in their lives. Each reveals that not only are there disjunctures between the ideology and practice of religion, but that women often negotiate and reinterpret religious dogma to their own advantage. Thus, for Jewish Orthodox women, enforced women-only spaces have become sources of strength and power for women. As Debra Kaufman notes of the women who participated in her study, "these women claim that their 'return' to the patriarchal setting of orthodoxy put them in touch with their own bodies, in control of their own sexuality, and in a position to value the so-called feminine virtues of nurturance, mutuality, family and mother-hood" (1991:8). Many Catholic charismatic women report that they find freedom in the gender roles prescribed by religious doctrine (Neitz, 1987). Fundamentalist women see themselves as fully participating agents in their marriages and religious communities (Ammerman, 1987). Women who subscribe to a conservative religious worldview see themselves as equal to, though different from, their husbands. There is some recognition of and desire to share in the male-dominated leadership positions; however, evangelical women also appreciate the women-only spaces they control as empowering and important.

Women who return to orthodoxy frequently report that their roles as mothers are valorized in their religious cultures, in contrast to secular society, which provides neither institutional nor ideological support for the mothering role. In addition, while there has been a tendency to focus on the control of women through conservative doctrine, women themselves accept as positive the conditions their religious beliefs impose on their husbands. While there is a perception that religious conservatism posits the male as a "boss" who can act unilaterally, most conservative approaches demand greater participation of men in family life, something that is not emphasized or supported in secular society. Moreover, Elizabeth Ozorak argues that while women often recognize their own inequality within church structures dominated by men, they also receive what to them are essential elements of the faith experience, specifically a feeling of connection and the enhancement of relationships (1996).

Although the limitations that patriarchal religious culture poses for women's actions are not dismissed by the researchers mentioned above, each recognizes the possibility of women's agency in the context of religious dogma, which might at one level seem to preclude independent action and thought. This research focuses on evangelical women and how they exercise agency through their interpretation of seemingly patriarchal religious dogma in their everyday lives. Some writers assume, with little more than anecdotal evidence, that submission in theory means that evangelical women are little more than doormats who exercise little or no agency. Yet there is a plenitude of evidence that suggests there is often a disjuncture between ideology and practice in religious contexts and that religious ideology is translated into practice in diverse ways within faith communities.

For example, research on birth control practices among Roman Catholics reveals that, despite explicit ideological prohibitions against contraception, which are regularly reinforced by pronouncements from the Vatican, Roman Catholics use a variety of birth control methods (Greely, 1993; Burns, 1996). Some Roman Catholic women have developed unique ways to express their faith within the Roman Catholic Church through "Women-Church," a coalition of Roman Catholic feminists (Trebbi, 1993; Ruether, 1983b). Similarly, the Catholic charismatic movement has risen within the context of mainstream Roman Catholicism as one expression of Catholic religious teachings. The charismatic movement within the Catholic church provides for its adherents a more meaningful framework for everyday living with a traditional backdrop, both reflecting and countering the modernist revisions of Vatican II (Neitz, 1987). At the other end of the spectrum, Catholic home-groups allow liberal Roman Catholics some respite from the conservative teachings of the church (Joyce, 1994).

Nancy Ammerman has found that fundamentalist Christians interpret church dogma in ways that make sense to adherents in their daily lives; while fundamentalists may not deviate far from church teachings, they do translate ideology in diverse ways (1987). James Davison Hunter points to the range of beliefs among evangelical Christians (1987b). It is also well recognized that there is often a divergence of opinion and approach between clergy and laity in churches, despite the fact that both are guided by the same ideology (Cohn, 1993; Alumkal, 1994). Ideological debates often become enmeshed in practical expressions of religion, sometimes causing a schism to the point of church or denominational divisions or splits (Ammerman, 1990; Warner, 1988).

Although I begin with the assumption that, for the most part, the women I talked to are religious practitioners within a patriarchal framework, I also assume that this does not preclude women's agency. This book focuses on how evangelical women build a life using their faith to order their lives. By exploring daily life, we can gain greater insight into how evangelical women use their religious worldview to make decisions and to explain their joys and their hardships. We will see evangelical women as agents who negotiate their own autonomy in their families, their churches, and in the world around them. Using everyday life as a beginning point, we can begin to understand the limits of accommodation and the shape of the boundaries between evangelicals and the world around them.

Agency-Structure

Under what conditions and by which processes do religious participants reinterpret religious structure? David Brown and Judith Kulig (1998) describe agency as the capacity of persons (individuals or collectives) to materially and symbolically produce, resist, transform, and reproduce the structures of their social worlds (defined more specifically as including "relational networks, distributions of control and systems of meaning") through action. These structures in turn enable and constrain human agency within particular contexts of social interaction. If we view structure as "relational networks, distributions of control and systems of meaning," a multifaceted conceptualization of structure is clearly necessary.

Nancy Ammerman (1997) argues, in her quest for a "more textured interpretation of human agency," that we need a new approach to the social scientific study of religion that is better able to capture the complexities of religious participation. Ammerman's postmodern approach involves a three-tiered analytic framework that places the religious actor in social and organizational context. She argues that we need to examine religious activity at the levels of the individual religious organizations, and the social context in which the religious activity takes place.

At the level of the individual, it is important to recognize that in a voluntaristic religious world, "no single organizational or belief context can explain any person's actions" (Ammerman, 1997:204). Thus, we should only use the term *religious worldview* broadly, not in a narrow, statically prescriptive sense. However, using Ammerman's understanding, simply because an evangelical woman describes herself as a feminist and participates in church activities less than a "traditional" evangelical woman does not mean she lacks commitment. In relation to commitment, Ammerman poses the question, "How and under what circumstances do persons enact religious behavior and how that behavior supports the goals of religious organizations and tunes individual sensibilities in religious directions?" (1997:206). What makes religious action possible? How are evangelical women able to sort through the rhetoric of submission and operationalize it in their daily lives? What are the complexities and contradictions in their negotiation of the tension between the demands of the church organization and the society in which they live? Each of these questions links back to the overall theme of structure and agency. Ammerman proposes two levels of structural analysis, always keeping in mind the individual as the beginning point of analysis.

At the level of religious collectivities, Ammerman emphasizes multidimensionality, which she attributes to the shifting collection of people who make up religious organizations. This is a particularly useful conceptualization of religious organizations given women's more extensive participation in and commitment to religious collectivities (Ozorak, 1996; Nason-Clark, 1993; Neitz, 1987). While women are, if not by policy then by practice, often excluded from positions of clerical leadership within evangelical churches, the religious collectivity is not only constraining for women, but it also opens the possibility for agency. Women use religious organizations as sites for individual and collective agency on multiple issues in a myriad of ways. In order to gain a more complete understanding of the lives of the women who participated in this study, we must examine not only their individual religious behaviors and beliefs, but how they are situated in a religious collectivity. In fact, the initial invitation to participate in the research was offered in the context of focus groups of church women, the vast majority of which took place in church buildings with groups of church women who met on a regular basis. However, as Ammerman points out, not all religious action takes place in the religious institution.

An analysis that sets up a binary opposition such as "religious institution" and "religious actor" as a rigid framework will inevitably fail to capture the complexities of religious practice. We need to consider the intersection of religious and community contexts as it is mediated by the social capital acquired by individuals within religious organizations. Ammerman identifies fellowship groups as breeding groups for social capital, or those basic relationships of trust between human beings. Thus, how do evangelical women bring their commitment to service to their workplaces, their support to abused women, their interactions with others while grocery shopping or at their children's sports events? A necessary aspect of this analysis is a consideration of the extent to which evangelical women appropriate secular ideologies to support their religious commitment and participation. How, for example, is feminism understood and used as a tool for dealing in the world?

Understanding how evangelicals maintain their beliefs in a secular world has been a source of debate among scholars, sparked by James Davison Hunter's (1991) descriptive metaphor of "culture wars." Hunter argues that there are conflicting, or more strongly, warring, moral visions of America, which he describes as orthodoxy, or "the commitment on the part of adherents to an external, definable and transcendent authority" (1991:44), and progressivism, which is "the tendency to resymbolize historic faiths according to the prevailing assumptions of everyday life" (1991:44). Hunter has been specifically criticized for failing to consider gender in this sweeping, and what some view as monolithic, portrayal of American society (Davis and Robinson, 1995). While evangelical women might contain a small subset of women who represent these two camps, it is not at all clear that such a sharp division is a useful way to analyze the agency-structure dynamic.

The way we think about the relationship between evangelicals and the secular world around them affects how we look at the third level of analysis proposed by Ammerman. Although evangelical women appropriate some secular ideologies, the line is not always clearly drawn between secular and sacred. Although they espouse a rhetoric of difference, which we will see in their discussions of marriage, there is not always a clear demarcation of the sacred/secular boundaries. It is as much the blurred lines as the sacred/secular wall that will be explored in the following pages. It is human agency and its impact on the shaping of social structure that continuously presents challenges to any sociological analysis of religious participation.

The voices we hear in this book add to our understanding of the complexities of how evangelical women translate their worldview into practice, taking into account their negotiations through church and the broader social structure in which they live. It is important to begin with the women themselves, and their articulations of their beliefs and practices as they struggle to make lives for themselves. From their stories we can identify themes that help us to see patterns in the agency-structure dynamic. The diversity of the voices, however, underscores a second point: Evangelical women are not a monolithic group. They exercise agency in different ways, in multiple sites, and in the complex dynamic of interlinking social structures described above.

This book explores the differences, as well as the similarities, among women who describe themselves as evangelical Christians. Like any group of women who subscribe to a common ideology, evangelical women are diverse. Although they are guided by conservative Protestant ideology, they are not monolithic in their response to it. There are three general categories into which evangelical women fall: traditionalists, moderates, and feminists. The first group of women are very traditional in their beliefs about women's roles—women are mothers and homemakers—and more literal in their interpretation of biblical prescriptions. This group might be characterized as fundamentalists, although they may not actually use that word to describe themselves. The second group, who make up the majority of evangelical women, are more moderate in their approach. They are less likely to subscribe to submission and headship without qualification, and they express a greater willingness to embrace feminism, although they are careful to distinguish themselves from extremists or from anything that might conflict with their Christian commitment. The third group, feminists, are more liberal in their interpretation of evangelical ideology. They are most likely to reject notions of headship and submission, seeing Christian marriages as partnerships with no need for lip service to those evangelical doctrines that can be interpreted to diminish women's equality. While not always, these women are most likely to call themselves evangelical feminists.

These categories, set out in greater detail in chapter 2, are loose and intended only as a broad characterization. For example, not all women who reject a literal interpretation of submission call themselves feminists. The point is that evangelical Christian women range from those who adhere to a traditionalist stance to those who are somewhat liberal in their interpretations of evangelical doctrines; yet each woman in the spectrum considers herself to be an evangelical Christian. While each of their approaches to the world could be considered "evangelical," they are clearly diverse. Evangelical women translate conservative Christian ideology in ways that help them to make sense of their own experiences as mothers, wives, volunteers, and members of the paid labor force. While that ideology can be conceptualized as a sacred canopy of meaning, it is not an all-encompassing shelter or determinative structure. Women's interpretation, reinterpretation, and interaction with their social context outside of the evangelical world and within their day-to-day lives changes the shape and color of the canopy such that it is not a static structure.

In the chapters that follow I will explore a variety of issues that are sites of tension in the agency–structure dynamic as it is situated in the individual, church, and society in general. How evangelical women think about and practice their faith illuminates the ways in which they reshape and reproduce social structure. The data is presented so that church women speak for themselves on their faith commitments, their marriages, their roles, feminism, and violence against women. In general, the book seeks to answer the question: What does it mean to be an evangelical woman?

2

Traditionalists, Feminists, and Moderates: Three Evangelical Portraits

Janice greets me at the door before I have even had a chance to ring the doorbell. She welcomes me into her living room. The house smells of potpourri and fresh baking. I sit on her pink and blue couch, which has hand-quilted accent cushions. There are coordinating cross-stitched wall hangings with Bible verses and little children. There are pictures of what I assume to be her children and a family picture on the end table beside my tape recorder with Janice, her husband, and their children. She comes into the room with a tray of coffee, freshly baked muffins, and what is clearly the good china. I feel honored that she has gone to this trouble for me, and I tell her so. She declares that it was no trouble at all, and she is just hopeful that she can tell me something useful for my research. She really doesn't know why I have chosen her—there must be other women who could be more helpful and who would know more than she does.

The attitude of humility and service Janice exudes in her self-presentation and the distinctive material culture evidenced in her home are characteristic of evangelical women. Wheeler's discussion of material culture had in some measure cued me to observe the material phenomenon of the evangelical world I immersed myself in. While the pervasiveness and form of this material culture varies, there is a distinctive decorating style that predominated in many of the homes I visited. It consisted of matching, country-style wallpapers, curtains, placemats, and chair cushions, often in roses and blues, together with numerous variations on the "wall hanging with Bible verse" theme, and in fact, "Bible cozies" were occasionally observed. Certainly not all evangelical homes are decorated in this manner, but having been in about seventy-five homes over the course of my fieldwork, this style did emerge in many homes on both a grand scale and in small ways. Wheeler argues that this vast and distinctive material culture of evangelical Christianity is part of the strength of conservative Protestant Christianity. It reminds evangelicals of who they are and serves as an identifying marker. It is also, as I will argue later, part of what evangelical women see as one of their primary duties in relation to their families, that of "setting the tone" (cf. Beaman and Nason-Clark, 1997b).

Evangelical women identify a distinct attitude or approach to life that they view as coming from their Christian commitment. Service and humility are central features of this attitude, and it pervades their daily life. Confident that God's will will be done, and that it will be in their best interests, evangelical women see selfishness and self-centeredness as un-Christlike. Although they are strong in their faith, the women I interviewed were not certain that they could tell a researcher anything of interest. As I came to know them, I realized that for the vast majority of women this was in no way explicable by a lack of reflexivity on their part, but reflected an attitude of humility pervasive among this group of women.

Kirby and McKenna stress that an egalitarian setting and relationship between the interviewer and the participant is critical (1989:67). Facilitating this relationship takes close attention to the cultural cues of a given group and can involve dress, language, and information sharing. For example, it quickly became apparent that my "conservative and dressy" approach to clergy interviews I had done for another research project in the same evangelical communities would not work in this study, so I modified my dress code to a more casual one in order to ensure that the women were not uncomfortable. I also wore a modest amount of makeup and conservative earrings so as not to risk offending any of the participants.

Since this research was located in the context of the research of the Religion and Violence Research Team at the Muriel McQueen Fergusson Center for Family Violence Research, and we had ongoing projects with evangelical Christians, gaining access to the conservative Protestant community was not difficult. Our team had conducted focus group research on violence and women, and at the end of those focus groups, participants were invited to take part in another study, involving individual interviews. The data in this book was collected from ninety-four evangelical[1] women in Atlantic Canada. Data was gathered through semistructured interviews that lasted from forty-five minutes to three hours, with the average interview being about ninety minutes. Most women were interviewed in their homes; the others were interviewed in various settings: at their places of employment, in their churches, at my motel, at the university, and in restaurants. In all cases the place of meeting was their choice, and a time convenient for them was scheduled.

If one were to listen to the interview tapes, they would, I think, air as easy conversations, frequently interspersed with laughter. I genuinely enjoyed meeting the women who participated in the research, and while many of them do not share my worldview, I admire their commitment to a worldview and a way of life that they sincerely believe makes the world a better place in which to live and themselves better prepared to meet the needs of others. For most of these women, Christianity is not a static commitment, but a dynamic, continuing struggle to meet the ideological standards of their faith while interacting in and making sense of a secular world.

The church communities from which these women came ranged from small, country churches with an approximate attendance of thirty on a given Sunday, to larger churches with congregations numbering in the hundreds. Most of the women were married (83 percent), with husbands they described as

---

[1]Sixty of the participants were United Baptist, twenty-nine were Wesleyan, and five were "other."

Christian. Participants ranged in age from twenty-three to seventy years of age, the average age being forty-four. Of the participants, 26 percent worked in part-time paid employment, 26 percent worked in full-time paid employment, 34 percent were full-time homemakers, two women were on disability leave, six were unemployed and looking for work, and six women were retired from the paid labor force. Their occupations were varied, ranging from professionals such as teachers and nurses (34 percent), to childcare workers (12 percent), sales clerks (13 percent), and self-employed in small and large businesses (10 percent). Only four of the women had not completed high school, 26 percent had attended community college or business school, 17 percent had some university or college, 27 percent had a bachelor's degree, and four women had master's degrees. Almost all had children, ranging in age from three months to forty-eight years of age. The vast majority used the label "evangelical" to describe themselves. These participants were an interesting mix of new (or "baby," as one interviewee described them) Christians, those who had been part of the evangelical community all of their lives, some who had switched from a more fundamentalist background, those who had grown up in a conservative Christian family, and women who had no Christian heritage.

The following composite pictures of three evangelical women represent the three types of women who participated in this study: traditionalists, moderates, and feminists. These categories emerged gradually, through the research process, and were not preconceived prior to the fieldwork. These typologies are based on gender role attitudes, which Gesch argues is strongly related to whether and how women are religious (1995:128).[2] The feminists and the traditionalists are at either end of the spectrum, each representing approximately 10 percent of the women who participated in this study. Demographic details and any identifying information have been altered to protect the identities of the women. The quotations are from actual interview transcripts. The use of these composites is intended to offer a textured picture of the lives of the three types of women as they talk about their faith and how it impacts on their daily negotiations in their families, churches, and the world. Obviously such

---

[2]In her study, Gesch found that most women were moderates, approximately one quarter were feminists, and 8 percent were traditionalists. Her sample was not limited to conservative Protestants.

typologies cannot capture the complexities of the lives of all evangelical women, but they are generally representative of the women in the three categories.

The composites have been constructed to reflect the differences between evangelical women in broadly conceptualized categories (see appendix A for a detailed description of the construction of these categories). For example, women differed in their interpretations of submission, their beliefs about women's participation in the paid labor force, their espousal of the tenets of feminism, and their discussions about roles in the family. Sometimes, their differences are in tone, rather than in practice. For example, women who declare that they believe women with small children should be full-time homemakers might have small children themselves and still work in the paid labor force. Submission may be wholeheartedly embraced, but only within very narrow parameters, which include equality in decision-making and a responsible husband. It is these disjunctures between ideology and practice, and the mediating factors between them, that are an important part of understanding evangelical women's lives.

Mary: An Evangelical Traditionalist

Mary meets me at the door of her bungalow in a rural area of Nova Scotia. She has baked muffins in honor of my visit, and two hours later when I leave her home she will send me away with two, expressing concern that I will not have a chance for a proper meal during my long day of traveling and interviewing. She offers me a pair of slippers because she has not built a fire and is afraid my feet will get cold. We talk about where we can most comfortably do the interview, and although Mary has set up the dining table for this purpose, she offers to move if that does not suit my needs. She has stacked the quilt pieces she is working on on a chair in the corner of the room. We talk a bit about how I have come to be interested in the research I am doing, and then we switch the focus to a discussion of the importance of her faith to her.

Mary is a sixty-eight-year-old widow who works part-time as a clerk at a local government office in order to make ends meet. Her husband died twenty years ago, leaving her to raise their three boys alone. When I ask her about her Christian commitment, she describes some of the miracles God has performed in her life. Her unswerving belief that God loves her stems from an experience she had many years ago, which she shares with me: "And I thought, Lord, you know, I have confessed to everything I know of, I repent, and I am truly sorry. And it just happened like—the song says 'sparks from smitten steel just so quick salvation reached me, praise God, I know it's real— it's real, it's real.' And that's just the way it was with me, beyond a shadow of a doubt, and that was years and years ago, and that's never left me." She is active in her church, as well as in a local interdenominational Bible study group.

In her comments about modern life, she is critical of parents who do not use physical punishment on their children and cites the biblical wisdom "Spare the rod and spoil the child." She says, "I think Christian parents or parents who really love their children shouldn't be reprimanded or put in jail because they discipline their children with a spanking—as long as the child isn't bruised." She is also critical of women who work outside the home for reasons other than absolute financial necessity. She notes that if women would stay at home, then perhaps there would be more jobs for men who have to provide for their families: "You know, if she wants to work at home, like make quilts or something like that, but I think it would make for a much happier home if she were home and it would make him feel good. He would feel 'I'm providing for my family.'" She worries about the effects of women in the workplace on men: "A man might feel inferior because perhaps her education, and you know, she may make a bigger salary and all kinds of things that tend to make her feel that she is the one who is running the show."

When we talk about submission, she is unequivocal in her support for male headship. Men are, in her view, God's intended leaders, and as such have the right to make the final decisions related to family life. Though women are weaker than men, they have a special role as God's caregivers and nurturers, and as such are "equal" to men. "I feel that the man should have a stronger, how should I put it?...well, he's the leader in the home and I just feel that...I know some homes a wife can balance the checkbook much better than the husband can, and so I think those things, I'm not saying he has to be the head of everything. But, I think when it comes to...well, like buying a new car—I want a certain kind, and he feels another kind would be more for our budget and more economical, so I think his word has to be the final word." To Mary, if women accept their role as helpmate, they will have a happy home, with no "pull as to who runs the show." Divorce, in her view, is simply not an option for Christians.

To Mary, Christian commitment is evidenced and witnessed through an unselfish attitude, which sometimes means letting someone else "have the advantage." Her day begins with prayer: "Prayer and praise—I always try to thank the Lord first thing in the morning for my night's rest and for this new day and ask for his help throughout the day." She doesn't watch "junk" on television, particularly anything with "cursing and swearing," she tries to eat in restaurants that don't serve liquor, and she tries to be considerate of others, although she acknowledges that there are considerate non-Christians as well.

Jane: An Evangelical Moderate

Jane races into her driveway in her minivan and jumps out, beckoning to me while she helps two children disembark. As she hustles them into the house, which is in a middle-income neighborhood in a small city, she tells me to make myself at home in the family room while she puts the children down for their naps. The home (or what I can see of it) is neat and nicely decorated, a fact that becomes incredible when Jane tells me that she has five children. Before she sits down to join me she invites me to join her in a glass of lemonade, and while she pours she tells me about her daughter's track and field meet, from which she has just come, and for which we have had to postpone the interview by a half hour. She apologizes for the delay, but explains that it was important for her to be there to support her daughter. It's a hot day, and Jane is dressed in a sleeveless tank top, shorts, and running shoes. She is wearing a modest amount of makeup. We begin the interview, and over the next two hours the two children who were napping reemerge and the three older children return home from school. Jane deals with each in turn, instructing them to change their clothes and telling them where the snacks are. The phone rings, and I overhear Jane negotiating her contribution to the church supper—two pies, fine, she can do that. During the course of the interview, Jane tells me how important being an evangelical Christian is to her; she doesn't know how people manage to get through life without Christ. "An evangelical to me means someone that's a little more intense about their Christianity, a little more excited about it, wanting to make it more than just a Sunday thing. I am not just interested in teaching my children Bible stories, but how they can have Christ as their personal Savior and Lord." For Jane, God is involved in every aspect of her life, including her marriage: "I firmly believe the circumstances in which Dan and I came together were such that we really feel that God brought us together." Her Christian worldview frames her life—most of her friends are Christian, she witnesses to her children, and she is extensively involved in her church: she sings in the choir, is involved in the missionary guild, attends Bible study, and participates in a couples group. She seeks the Lord's guidance and forgiveness through prayer on a daily basis and she feels comforted by her personal relationship with Jesus: "It gives me comfort knowing that God cares about me and my husband and my children, and it makes me feel assured that anything that is going to happen is not outside His realm of control, so it just gives me peace that whatever comes my way then I know that God already knew about it first, and that He is there to support me."

Jane says that although she understands that some women want or need to work outside the home, for her it is simply not a desirable option, and, with five children, not really a choice at all. She sees herself as being very lucky to have a supportive husband who earns a good income. She is comfortable in her role as "just" a homemaker: "I stay at home, and the reason I stay at home is because Dan and I decided before we were married that we were going to have a big family, and we both knew that I wanted to be home. He wanted me home, but even before he told me he wanted me home I said, you know, I would be home. That was the home that we had grown up in, our Moms had been home. I never even thought of anything other than that and neither had he." They have just come back from a rare escape weekend, and she sees the recent time by themselves as valuable. Jane is uncomfortable with feminism because she feels that feminists promote too much of their own agenda and not enough of God's.

Although her evangelical husband is head of their household, and she would describe herself as a submissive wife, decisions are always made jointly. She thinks that men have the more difficult biblical role: "I have had some discussions with women who have a real difficult time with that—'Wives submit to your husbands.' Now I don't have difficulty with that at all, because in the next breath it says 'Husbands love your wives as Christ loved the church.' In my mind, we've got the easy end of the job, they've got the hard one. I mean, they've got to love like Christ. If they love like Christ, it can't be difficult to submit to that. I mean, that's perfect love."

Beth: An Evangelical Feminist

Beth is a thirty-six-year-old nurse and mother of two small children. I arrive at her house a bit earlier than scheduled, but she is very welcoming. Her house is in a suburb of a small city. She has just returned from Bible study. Beth works part-time and says that she would not be happy unless she was in the labor force. "I don't want to be just here and just thought of as a mother, although I think that's a very important job, and I want to do it the best I can, but I want to have other interests outside of that role." Her part-time status allows her the best of two worlds—time to spend with her children, and an opportunity to remain active in her profession. Her husband is a firefighter and works shift work, so he is often able to spend time with their children. In fact, as I am interviewing Beth he comes home at the end of his shift and makes lunch for the children. Though she grew up in a Christian home, Beth does not feel that her real commitment to Christ happened until her mid-twenties. She describes herself as an evangelical Christian. She feels that "as a woman, it's our duty to promote the gospel when we have opportunity to present it to people if they are willing to receive it." She attends church regularly and is also involved in two church groups, one of which is the Thursday morning women's Bible study where I first met her. She tells me that since my research team visited her women's group, she has started praying for abused women. While she feels that her life is church-centered, she does have many non-Christian friends. She is troubled by the Godless society she feels we are becoming.

When I raise the issue of submission, Beth declares that she does not buy into "that submission stuff." She explains that she is an equal partner in her marriage and is unwilling to call her husband "the head" of their household. "We are both the head," she declares, and their household is run as a "team effort." She says, "Baptists are so brought up in the fact that the man is the

head of the home and the head of the house and what he says
goes. And that's changing more and more, I think in the younger
women today, that it's not considered, it's you, you really should
consider God the head of your home, and you two are an equal
team." She refers to marriage as a "covenant" with God as well
as one's spouse, although she believes there are times when
separation and divorce are acceptable. She says that although a
lot of people would describe her as a feminist, and she would
describe herself as one, "I don't really feel I'm a true feminist
because I like to stay at home, and I like to take care of my children,
and I get a lot of enjoyment out of that, but I also like to be in the
work force too." She is grateful for the feminist movement and
the advances she feels it has brought for women.

The stories reveal both differences and similarities between evangelical women: For all of them, faith is central to their lives. Evangelical women use their faith as a reference point for their daily lives, which is the site for the complex interaction of agency and structure. They pray about difficulties in their lives and in the lives of their friends and families; they consult with Christian friends; they model a Christian lifestyle in the workplace. Each of the women is active in her church. But to talk about "the" evangelical worldview is misleading. While evangelicalism cannot be reduced to a relativistic amalgam of individual interpretations, it is mediated by individual actors.

What differentiates between evangelical women are the ways in which they as individuals mediate structural influences. Patterns in these differences allow us to develop broad categories within which women exercise agency—as feminists, traditionalists, or moderates. For example, church doctrine on submission is redefined in the context of individual marital relationship and family life. Feminist evangelicals appropriate secular feminism to redefine and reject some aspects of the religious structure. In a somewhat less than usual evangelical approach to the Bible, Beth says:

When the Bible was interpreted it was so much of the...of the times. So much of that was brought into the scriptures, and it can't help not being because the people that wrote the scriptures...were living in these times, and this is what they knew, and it was so acceptable, and it was the norm. And people imply that you have to be like that today, and I just don't believe that we do.

However, unlike Beth, even though evangelical traditionalists espouse submission, translated and mediated, this acceptance is practiced as equality within their marital relationships. Traditionalists are not mousy doormats, but independent agents who negotiate submission in ways that preserve and promote their individuality and freedom as agents and as equals in their relationships. If we look at Mary's example of her husband's exercising final authority—the purchase of a new vehicle—we could argue that on issues that are not important to her, she deferred to her husband. But in her conversations she remembers her relationship with her husband as a joint struggle to raise their children and to meet the challenges of daily life with the support of the Lord. Thus, although a simplistic analysis might conclude that traditionalists simply reproduce the dogma of submission, they reinterpret it in ways that refocus the teaching to mutuality and equality. Obviously this begs the question of why pay lip service to the rhetoric of male headship, but evangelical traditionalists themselves would reject a characterization of their agency as subverting the "true" meaning of submission and headship. For moderates like Jane, submission *means* equality, and such equality is biblically based. In the view of moderates, the Bible advocates mutuality in submission, not lordship. In her day-to-day life, Jane sees herself as a part of a team effort with her husband to model and live a Christian commitment.

A similar deconstruction needs to be carried out in relation to evangelical women's participation in the paid labor force. Lyn Gesch argues that a woman's gender role orientation affects the extent to which she is likely to be involved in church-related activities. She points out that what "women think about their 'proper' roles tends to be closely tied to their actual work and family activities" (1995:124). Some women, however, after entering the paid labor force find that they enjoy their work (Nason-Clark, 1993). Linking gender role orientation and church participation is a complicated task—it is a bit like asking which came first, the working mother or the feminist, and which impacts on church activity, feminism or the fact that a woman is working in the paid labor force? Moreover, if we return to Ammerman's conceptualization of religious participation, we need to ask questions about participation and church activity. If a working evangelical woman has minimal involvement in church activities, but raises her children to pray and read their Bibles regularly, and ensures that the family lifestyle is a Christian one, can she be considered to be any less committed than the woman who spends many hours immersed in church activities? Is such an analysis useful?

We can learn a great deal from Gesch's careful research, which highlights the complexity of studying religious participation. As a group, evangelicals are a complex amalgam of new and old Christians, women with varying educations and experiences. Evangelicals, too, are part of the voluntaristic, religious society we find ourselves in, and while we have often used the wall metaphor to think about how conservative Christians are in the world, it may be more useful to pay closer attention to the detailed nuances of religious participation, even with groups who may at first glance seem to be more immersed or more enveloped in the sacred canopy than others.

Women's involvement in church activities reproduces the organizational structure of the church in ways that reinforce the patriarchal male hierarchy of church leadership. For the most part, conservative Protestant women do not question or challenge the predominantly male clerical leadership. Why? In part it may be because they find fulfillment in the roles that are open to them. However, for Mary, the explanation is likely tied to the biblically prescribed role of men as leaders, in both the home and the church. For Jane, male leadership in the church is not necessarily God-ordained, but is simply how things are. For Beth, male leadership is simply another manifestation of patriarchy within the church. She represents the small group of women who do argue for women's presence in all aspects of church leadership. Other research we have done makes it obvious that in most cases male clergy simply "let" women's groups do their thing and have no idea what actually happens in the context of those groups on a meeting-by-meeting basis (Nason-Clark and Beaman-Hall, 1993a). For women, church provides a context in which they are nurtured and in which they can reach out to others. While there is some evidence that suggests that women are socialized to see their roles in the church as extensions of their roles in the home, this argument can work only to a limited degree because many evangelical women have responsibility for the financial management of their households, even when they do not earn an income. Thus, their exclusion from financial leadership within their churches is not simply a "logical" leap.

For each of the women introduced at the beginning of this chapter, the role of mother provides a vehicle through which faith is both lived out and transmitted. Yet for Mary, who is adamant about women's roles in the workplace (they shouldn't be there!), she has had to live a reality that is quite distinct from the religiously-based rhetoric she supports. Her participation in the paid labor force was out of necessity brought on by her husband's death, which left her as a single parent of a young family. As a moderate, Jane is supportive of the idea of women in the paid labor force but finds fulfilment for herself in her role as a stay-at-home mother. This, too, is partly out of necessity, because of the size of her family. Beth both supports the participation of women in the paid labor force and lives it out through her part-time participation in it. Yet, no matter what their choice, each woman (for those who have children) sees mothering as a central and important part of her life.

The focus on mothering leads to some interesting comparisons between evangelical women and radical feminists. Debra Kaufman contrasts Orthodox Jewish women and radical feminists and points out that the similarities are often striking. However, the key difference is the apolitical position of Orthodox women. Similarly, evangelical women valorize women's roles as mothers and as caretakers. They extend this caring role in the nurturing they do in their church and secular communities. However, unlike feminist celebrations of women's unique abilities, evangelical women do not use women's differences as political leverage. Rather, those differences are most often used as evidence for continued separate spheres of responsibility for men and women.

What are the differences between moderates, traditionalists, and feminists? Each group frames their experiences within an evangelical framework, but there is diversity in boundary negotiation and the agency-structure dynamic. Traditionalists are most likely to choose to accept the rhetoric of the church and yet find ways to practice it in their daily lives in a way that preserves their autonomy and maximizes their own agency. They emphasize separation from the world and work to preserve boundaries between their sacred canopy and the world around them. Moderates choose to interpret church doctrine in ways that promote their equality and seek to find ways to mediate between their evangelical worldview and the secular world. Feminists reject rhetoric that they see as being contrary to women's equality. They are unwilling to "stretch" the interpretation of such rhetoric to include an equality message. Women identify, interpret, and negotiate the boundaries of their faith in complex ways that reflect their own agency and their multilayered identities. The women I have chosen to represent each category do not fit "neatly." Such is the reality of women's lives. How would Jane have negotiated her workforce participation if she did not have five children? If Mary's husband had not died at an early age, leaving her a single mother, could she have lived out her belief that women should not "take" men's jobs? The categories are fluid, their boundaries flexible. We can, however, begin this exploration with the following assumption: The women within these categories describe themselves as evangelical. They see themselves as committed Christians, with a worldview that is distinct from those who do not know Jesus as their personal savior.

3

God's Hands and Feet

Mary talks about the importance of her faith to her as we sit curled up in comfortable armchairs in her living room. She tells me that while she has a difficult time talking to strangers about her testimony, she tries to model a Christian way of life, based on service to God and to others. She feels that this is as effective as telling people about Christ, or, as she puts it, "shoving the Bible down people's throats." She describes herself as "God's hands and feet." To her, the motto of Christian commitment is service—epitomized in the JOY formula—Jesus, others, then you.

Although the term *evangelical* is used by academic researchers to describe a particular religious group, those who are themselves evangelical are rarely asked to talk about what that term means to them. How do conservative Protestant women make sense of the term *evangelical*? What does it mean to them to call themselves evangelical Christians? Although witnessing to others is an important aspect of evangelical Christianity, beliefs and practices play an important role in defining the evangelical worldview. Service to God, others, and one's community is the key aspect that differentiates evangelicals from others. The ways in which

37

evangelical women understand their differences from those around them reflects their agency in relation to their social context. By distinguishing themselves, they mark the boundaries between themselves and the world around them. As we will see, moderates, traditionalists, and feminists establish their evangelical identities in different ways.

Sharing the Word

Sharing the word of God and the message of salvation is a central tenet of evangelical Christianity. As this woman enthusiastically put it:

> It means I love Christ so much and He's done so much for me I can't shut up about it, so I've got to let people know. (interviewee #56, age 33)

This thirty-three-year-old homemaker clearly felt a strong sense of obligation to share the salvation message with others:

> I guess I don't want to keep things to myself, I am…Christ has affected my life, and decisions that I've made, the roads that my husband and I have taken, and I've seen peace, and a conviction that that is not out of my own strength, ah, and all that Christ has done throughout my life, and I think that everybody is searching these days, um, why would I not want to share that? (#55)

Interestingly, the ideal of "sharing the good news" does not always translate into practice. This woman's statement reflects her reluctance to evangelize:

> It [evangelical Christian] means to me someone who is willing and able to share the gospel with others. I'm willing yes, I guess, I think I'm willing, but I don't think I'm that able. I know someone would have to confront me and ask me questions about it. (#46, age 27)

At least in part, the unease with sharing the gospel with others in an assertive way is connected to a dislike of pushiness, aggressiveness, or extremism (a theme that recurs again with many of these women when they talk about feminism). Evangelical women are conscious of the tendency of outsiders to see them as "fanatics" and are careful to distance evangelicalism from fundamentalism or "right wing" thinking, insisting that a love of

Jesus does not mean "shoving the Bible down people's throats." This thirty-two-year-old nurse stated:

> As a woman it's our duty to promote the gospel and when we have opportunity and present it to people, if they're willing to receive it...and um...if somebody is not interested then I'm not somebody that would push it on anybody in any respect, but if an opportunity came up, then...then I would talk about it. (#48)

Like the fundamentalists in Ammerman's study, evangelism for the women in this study is often something to which they subscribe but do not practice to the letter, at least in its narrowest definition of "telling" others. Though they recognize the importance of evangelism, women shape it to mean more than simply telling others to include witnessing through their lifestyle.[1]

> My husband and I go down to [a neighboring city] for supper; we'll often get up and have a nice waltz when they are playing the piano music. I think there is absolutely nothing wrong with that. But on the other hand we wouldn't do that in [the city in which she lives] for our witness' sake. Because there are people who think that there is something wrong with it. If somebody told me that, um, somebody in the church had a glass of wine with a meal, that wouldn't upset me at all, but if I walked into a restaurant and saw...I would think, for their witness' sake they shouldn't be doing it. (#1)

But evangelizing is only one part of the evangelical worldview; modeling a love of Christ through their everyday lives serves as a testimony or witness to their Christian commitment, as is illustrated by this thirty-five-year-old stay-at-home mother of three:

> Whenever I hear "evangelical" I think of someone up front, talking, preaching. I guess I'm not a preacher in that sense, but I...I do feel that my life and the way I conduct it is...is a testimony in that sense. (#45)

---

[1]Bibby's recent study of evangelical leaders suggests that while there is much talk of evangelizing, the actual number of "converts" is quite low. Bibby reports: "The actual number of 'outsiders' that our sample of 20 Calgary churches succeeded in recruiting averaged 1.3 between 1966 and 1970, 2.6 for 1976–1980, and 2.9 for 1986–1990." (1995:52)

The action component of evangelicalism includes the idea that one's Christian commitment should be demonstrated in everyday life, and involve both reaching out to others and holiness aspects such as abstention from alcohol.

> I think the…sometimes I think of the holiness aspect, like we abstain from alcohol or drugs, or…I don't know, we try to be Christlike, that's the idea—in everything, though sometimes we slip—we're not perfect. (#59, age 46)

The essence of evangelizing is sometimes described as acting as "God's hands and feet." Less public behaviors, such as prayer, are also central to their conceptualization of evangelicalism, in that prayer that others may come to Christ is a regular part of women's evangelizing.

Beliefs and Practices

For many conservative Protestants, being a Christian involves a particular set of beliefs and practices, as well as a lifelong commitment that is central to one's way of life, both in how one chooses to act and in how one interprets daily events.

> It's faith and belief in God, He is my maker, my creator, that He sent His son to die for me so that I could live with Him one day…it's a lifetime commitment to serve God as best you can. (#46, age 27)

Although most of the women who mentioned belief as a central aspect of evangelical Christianity frame it as belief in Christ, others focus on theological aspects of evangelism, such as the trinity, and the existence of heaven and hell. Although their worldview is scripturally based, this is not always specifically articulated. Rather, one finds verses, or bits of verses, interjected into conversation.

For some women, not only belief in Christ, but coming to that belief through a conversion experience, is an important aspect of their faith. There was a great deal of variety in their discussions of their own conversion among the participants, often depending on whether they had been raised in a Christian home or whether they had experienced a dramatic event in their own lives that "brought them to Christ." The conversion experience not only serves to mark a new life for the believer, but it also builds a wall between sacred and secular worlds. The shape and strength of this wall is flexible, and indeed the usefulness of such an analogy is questionable. For the most part, evangelicals negotiate the boundaries between themselves and the secular world, rather than build walls.

Markers of these boundaries also include overt behaviors directly related to religious practice, such as church attendance, prayer, and devotions. These involve negotiation with organizational demands that place a priority on public support. Difference is also manifested in lifestyle choices, such as abstinence from alcohol, keeping Christian company, and being less materialistic. Christian women have a sense of responsibility to present a good Christian image as a part of their witness.

To conservative Protestant women, being an evangelical Christian is central to their identities, and yet their descriptions of evangelical ideology and their adherence to religious doctrine do not involve an overt emphasis on evangelism. However, although they are uncomfortable "sharing the word" or "shoving the Bible down people's throats," they mediate the directive to evangelize in their own lives by reformulating it as a call to action, which impacts both on their actions in relation to others and their own behavior. Witnessing is thus translated as a way of life, the hallmark of which is service to others. Modeling the Christian life to others is seen as the most effective tactic for witnessing.

Evangelical women are passionate about their commitment to a Christian way of life. For them, Christianity is not inhibitive, but rather provides both prescriptions and explanations for daily life, which free them from the dilemmas faced by those who do not have the benefit of a "personal relationship with Jesus Christ." To outsiders, the boundaries within which conservative Christians strive to live often seem restrictive and stifling. But for those who live within them, the boundaries provide guidance and support in a complicated modern world.

Key to evangelical women's perceptions of their own lives is the idea that their faith provides the central pillar of support for both day-to-day living and times of crisis. Not all women experience the benefits of a Christian worldview in the same way. Many reflect on the difference their faith makes in terms of benefits to themselves, such as peace, having a friend (God or Jesus) to whom they can turn and who will support them, hope, and happiness. For some, Christianity provides a coping mechanism for life's difficulties:

> Well, it's like a ninety-degree thing, because when I am feeling down, I'm feeling bitter, or anything at all, I just, I just talk to the Lord and I just ask Him for help, and you know, before I know it, I have a different attitude, a different feeling. (#61, age 64)

However, the difference is manifested both in the impact on the women's own lives and on the lives of those who come into contact with them, whether within their families or with strangers. Many women talk about the ways in which Christian commitment has resulted in a greater concern for others, and less selfishness, which is sometimes articulated as a commitment to God and to do God's work. As one woman put it, she strives to ensure that her daily activities are to the glory of God.

Another woman, who described her dramatic conversion experience, said:

> It makes a big difference—when I wake…I wake up every morning…I became a Christian sixteen years ago, and every morning, and I can't say…I'm not exaggerating when I say, every morning I wake up, and I remember that God is real. And I think, let's get at it, this is a great day! No matter what takes place in my life, or…like my life's not perfect, that's for sure, God is real. (#67, age 47)

To this group of women, being a Christian is central to their everyday lives; as they describe it, Christianity gives them a purpose, makes their lives worthwhile, gives them a different outlook, and in many ways makes them totally different people. Some women said they simply couldn't imagine their lives without God.

For evangelical Christians, faith makes a difference not only in terms of reinforcement of internal strength, but also in terms of external markers of difference. To them Christianity makes a difference in their lives by fortifying their own strength and by giving them an outward focus, which mandates service to others as an important part of Christian life and Christian witness. They also see the practical impact of their beliefs in terms of the specifically religious rituals they incorporate in the daily routines of life, and their behaviors, such as abstinence from alcohol, which indicate to "the world" that they are different.

Some women are so immersed in their worldview that they have difficulty articulating how their faith makes a difference in their lives, a problem that seemed to arise not from a denial that their Christian commitment does make a difference, but that being an evangelical Christian is so integral to who they are that they were unable to express the differences in words.

Shaping Boundaries

The construction of boundaries is central to the establishment of a religious worldview that both explains everyday occurrences and prescribes appropriate actions in the everyday lives of adherents. For evangelical women, these boundaries are in part established through their belief that a Christian commitment does in fact make a difference in their lives, both in terms of the benefits to themselves and in their attitudes and actions in their relationships with others.

The creation and maintenance of boundaries facilitates the sense of group identity shared by evangelical Christians. Such boundaries have been conceptualized in a variety of ways by those who study tensions between religious groups and secular society. Ammerman talks about "negotiation" between fundamentalists and the world around them, as does Donald Kraybill in his analysis of the Amish (1989). Hunter builds conceptual walls he characterizes as a "culture war." In what sense do evangelicals negotiate boundaries, and how do they maintain walls? If we examine the three groups of women—moderates, traditionalists, and feminists—there are distinctions in the ways that each group negotiates its relationship with the world. Feminists do not see themselves as pitted against the world in a culture war, but rather see tensions and places for cooperation between evangelicals and those who hold other beliefs. Similarly, although the moderates see themselves as being different, they are "moderate" in their portrayal of differences. They seek ways to mediate the differences between themselves and others. The wall analogy, or Hunter's notion of culture wars, likely works best with the traditionalists. They see themselves as being starkly different from the secular world, and they want to keep it that way.

While conservative Protestant Christians live in mainstream society, they often strive to distinguish themselves from it through the development of their own distinctive culture, which includes material aspects (Wheeler, 1996), beliefs, and practices. The challenge is to live in the world but not to be dominated by it. Evangelicals accomplish this by immersing themselves in their own world as much as possible. Where feasible, many evangelical Christians go to Christian businesses, have Christian friends, and read Christian literature (Ammerman, 1987).

What do evangelical women identify as the differences between themselves and those in the secular world? There are obvious distinctions related to religious practice, described by the following woman as keeping God as the focus:

> [R]ead your Bible, and so sort of devotion, like you are constantly aware that just being good isn't enough, you have to pray, you have to be close to Him, and make sure you put Him first, you have to keep working at it. (#59, age 46)

One frequently cited difference is that of "attitude" or "outlook." Some women described non-Christian lives by making comparisons with their own lives. This woman felt lucky to be a Christian[2]:

> …Being a Christian, you always have hope, and a lot of non-Christians do cope with things too, you know, they cope, and I often wonder how people do, without knowing the Lord, you know. (#61, age 64).

Like this woman, many of the women I talked to perceived a difference in attitude or approach between themselves and non-Christians, particularly in relation to hope, peace, and a positive outlook. For evangelical Christians, this difference in attitude emanates from at least two sources: the knowledge that God is in control and the knowledge of their own salvation. This talk of attitude permeated the interviews, and yet it was difficult to identify how exactly it is manifested. For women, it is a double-edged sword. While a positive outlook is described as an advantage associated with being a Christian, it also puts pressure on evangelical women to present a "happy face."

---

[2]Although they were not specifically asked about the differences between Christians and evangelical Christians, the interview data suggests that for the vast majority of these women the word *Christian* means evangelical Christian, with its attendant boundaries.

Because well, ah…I suppose they think, well, I'm a Christian and I'm supposed to be able to solve my problems if I take them to the Lord, type thing. And ah…sometimes you think, well, I'm a Christian, I shouldn't have these problems in the first place, and ah…we do that even if we don't have those kinds of problems. It's ah…kind of …one of those things, I guess. We're supposed to have it all together maybe, but yet we're human and we forget that. (#7, age 41)

Another woman linked this pressure for perfection specifically with family life:

I think Christians are more vulnerable within a church setting because there's this pie in the sky type of attitude, where Christians are expected to be a certain way and do a certain thing, um, marriages are supposed to succeed. Ah, they're supposed to be examples, there's no room for failures, and when you do fail there's no place to go within the church structure to get help on an emotional, physical level. It seems like they're busy caring about the spiritual needs, and that is, that's fine, I'm not, I'm not condemning that. But what about the people who, who are already fallen that need help and they don't dare come out? It, it's like, it's like ah, fallen Christians that, that, that don't, they don't dare come out of the closet. It's like a disease or something. (#36, age 37)

A content analysis of one evangelical publication also revealed that evangelicals strive to be different or set apart from the secular culture in which they live (Beaman-Hall, 1994). Many of the articles centered around themes of faith and hope and included discussions of the joys of the authors' individual relationships with God. To these conservative Protestants, being a Christian helps them to cope with hard times, but also provides rewards in terms of a more fulfilling life (and hope for the afterlife). The emphasis on the importance and necessity of witnessing to others also underscores this theme, as do the numerous discussions of holiness. Clearly, the Christian way of life is perceived to be both better and different from the lifestyle and worldview adopted by non-Christians.

The idea that Christians are different also contributes to the downplaying of problems that are normally associated with the secular world. There is a certain amount of shame associated with the existence of abuse (or other social problems, for that matter) in the Christian family. This shame or embarrassment is illustrated in the articles reviewed for the content analysis by the fact that articles dealing with "personal" experiences of homosexuality, teenage pregnancy, and a child's drug abuse were anonymously authored.[3]

Women present the public face of the family—they are seen as being responsible for their children, and to some extent, for their husbands. In their words, they "set the tone." The pressure to be perfect is especially overwhelming for families in which there are problems such as child or wife abuse. In reaching out to others, Christian women sometimes ignore their own needs.

The theme of selfishness frequently emerges as an important dividing line between a life committed to Christ and one that is not. In their interactions with others, Christian women try to demonstrate the love of God by showing love and compassion, in the way they talk to others, and generally by being what they describe as less self-centered. While it is frequently recognized that non-Christians often do good works for others, they are often described as self-centered and not concerned with the needs of others, a factor that is mentioned as distinguishing a Christian life from that of the non-Christian. A selfless attitude is seen as being important to a Christian witness.

> I sort of think that…just a conversation I had with a non-Christian sister-in-law one time, saying that she couldn't make her family happy if she wasn't happy. And I sort of said, "I think that you've got that backwards. The way you are happy yourself is to make other people happy." And she couldn't relate to that. (#1)

Many women seemed to be uncomfortable with the dividing line I had chosen (Christian/non-Christian), and I frequently heard comments like, "Well, only God knows what is in a person's heart."

---

[3]The only other article to be anonymously authored discussed the tendency for people to focus on their clothing and their friends rather than worship when at church.

In our discussions of various people with whom they had contact, I sometimes asked, "Was that person a Christian?" The responses were either an unequivocal yes or a hesitant assessment in which the participant would say something like, "Well, she goes to church once in a while, but I don't think she has a personal relationship with Christ." While they had very often expressed clear ideas about what leading a Christian life means, evangelical women were also reluctant to be judgmental of those they thought might be living on the edge of Christian life.

I often heard comments which, like that of the following seventy-year-old retired woman, expressed pity for the non-Christian, asking, "How do they cope?":

> Well, the non-Christian does not have the knowledge, the understanding that they can call on God. Even, even people who aren't Christians pray, and God, I'm sure, answers some of their prayers. He always answers the prayer for salvation, but ah, well, I've said more than once, and I've heard other people say, "I don't know how a person who is not a Christian can face what some of them have to face." (#60)

The importance of God's support was a theme often reflected in the women's comments. The fact that Christians are not alone, that they can turn to God for support, and the knowledge that "he" is taking care of them are factors that, in the view of these women, distinguish the lives of evangelical women from their secular counterparts.

How does the perception that one's strength is rooted in God, rather than in oneself, impact on how women think about their own agency? Evangelical women strike a balance between themselves as self-actualizing selves and submissive servants to God. But even in their recognition of God's power in their lives, women leave room for their own agency. While they seek and pray for guidance, their choices are ultimately their own.

In her study of Christian schools, Melinda Wagner points out that conservative Protestant Christians are neither individualistic nor collectivist; rather they are Christ-centered, or "christocentric." According to Wagner, the ideological boundaries of conservative Protestantism are defined by christocentrism, in which the primary unit of reference is Christ (1990). Evangelical women, though they find support in church groups and, more particularly, in other church women, clearly define their lives in relation to their commitment to Christ. They are in constant communication with God in their everyday lives, seeking guidance and approval for their choices. To them, their commitment to serving others is a manifestation of their commitment to serve Christ. It is this christocentric approach that distinguishes evangelical women from non-Christians.

For evangelical women, describing themselves as different is part of the process of articulating boundaries between their world and the secular world. Though that difference is reflected in public practices such as going to church services and other church-related activities, it is also manifested in private behaviors like prayer and devotion. However, equally as important in defining the difference between evangelical Christians and those who do not share their worldview is an attitude, an approach to the world that involves putting others first, a peace that emanates from the belief that God is there to turn to, and a sense of purpose through the devotion of one's life to the "work of the Lord."

How does the commitment to service and an outward focus relate to activism by evangelical women? As is the case among other groups of evangelicals (Hunter, 1987b), the approach to activism was a particularly sensitive issue among this group of conservative Christian women. When women talk about the problems in the world that most trouble them, one common theme is violence against women. Interestingly, while they minimize the help they offer to abused women, evangelical women are extensively involved in providing support to victims of family violence. They listen, offer material resources such as food, clothing, and money, and they provide shelter and baby-sitting services. While they may not mobilize politically, evangelical women are activists on the front line of service provision.

Less predominant than one might think, given the emphasis in popular culture on conservative Protestantism's preoccupation with family, were responses related to the breakdown of the family (only three women mentioned family values in response to this question). While a number of participants were worried about children, only one woman framed this in the context of the breakdown of the family. Equally surprising given the association of conservative Protestant Christians with anti-abortion activism is the infrequent mention of abortion. A number of women mentioned their support for anti-abortion groups, but one woman mentioned abortion as the social problem that most troubles her in the world today. Several women mentioned the lack of respect for human life, but they did not specifically contextualize it in relation to the abortion issue. Identifying selfishness as a problem also emerges in their discussion of problems in the world; evangelical women are troubled by what they see as the modern-day world's focus on self-interest and self-indulgence.

The characterization of themselves as outwardly focused and the portrayal of "the world" as selfish is one way in which evangelical women reinforce boundaries and the notion that they are "in the world, but not of it." Through their own agency—selfless acts of service—they are able to create distance between themselves and what they see as the dominant message of the secular world—love thyself.

When I asked them whether they were activists on the problem they named, most participants denied outright any activism. But when I probed further, they admitted that they prayed about the issue, that they were involved in local and sometimes international agencies that dealt with the problem, they provided financial support to relief agencies and groups, and they were certainly vocal about the issue with their families and friends. This sixty-four-year-old's response is representative of those made by many of the women I interviewed:

> I guess I don't do too much, really…I can't say that I do. Well, you know, I have a foster child, and in India, and our auxiliary group, we support several foster children, our women's missionary society are reaching out funds, to…financially, and support like Operation Eyesight, and these things, and food bank, I always support the food bank, and I…started out with Meals on Wheels, you know…I don't see anything concrete that I personally am doing over and above…you wish you could do something that would be a little more…I give to the Sharing Way, and I know they're in there working with all this, but it doesn't seem like enough. And I know there are poor around us, we give to the food bank, but we're not really doing too much for them otherwise. (#38)

While most of the participants seemed to have an aversion to describing themselves as activists, it was perhaps the connotations of extremism in that word that caused them to minimize their involvement in social issues, rather than a lack of commitment to changing the world in which they live.

Although evangelical women may be reluctant to see or to describe themselves as activists, they do acknowledge their commitment to service. In their descriptions of what it means to be an evangelical, these women highlighted selflessness and attitude toward others. This fifty-one-year-old school teacher's comment summarizes the centrality of an "other-focused" attitude:

> [Y]ou don't just go to church on Sunday, but you try to live as you believe the Lord would want you to, and that means we often use children's programs and so on, the three-letter word JOY—Jesus first, others in the middle, and yourself last. So you are not selfish. You think of others. (#52)

In their differentiation of themselves from non-Christians, again the theme of service to others emerges. In their reflections about how being an evangelical Christian makes a difference in their lives, these women talked about thinking of others first. Their identification of problems in the world includes a consideration of selfishness. For evangelical women, their faith provides direction and meaning to their lives, while at the same time differentiating them from non-Christians and the secular world. From their point of view, the highlight, and indeed the hallmark, of Christian life is service to others. The call to evangelize is mediated by evangelical women such that it is translated into an everyday modeling of their faith through service and "setting a good example." Their church-related activities again highlight service to others through leadership, caring for children, and responsibilities related to church functioning. This "ethic of service" may emerge in part from what many women see as their primary function in their families, and indeed in their lives—that of mothering.[4]

---

[4]Debra Kaufman noted a similar link in her study of Orthodox Jewish women. She says: "The social practices associated with nurturance dominate their lives" (1991:125).

4

Ministering to Family

Well, I'm the caregiver, and I find the woman sets the mood. She really does; 'cause if the woman is upset, everybody can get upset so quick and so easy, so I have to keep my calm [she laughs]. It's not easy sometimes. (#71, age 42)

Evangelical writings about and prescriptions for family life are often modeled on ideas about the "traditional" family, a model that Hunter argues is really an "idealized form of the nineteenth-century middle-class family: a male-dominated nuclear family that both sentimentalized childhood and motherhood and, at the same time, celebrated domestic life as a utopian retreat from the harsh realities of industrial society" (1991:180; see also Balmer, 1994). Within conservative Protestant culture there is little room for family models that fall outside of heterosexual relationships, but some flexibility about appropriate roles for men and women is apparent.

Based on nineteenth-century notions of the "delicate" and "morally superior" nature of women, present-day fundamentalist views about women's roles center around the home and their position as the guardians of that which is most precious, their children. Real women are feminine, stay-at-home mothers, who focus on the needs of their children and their husbands. But there

51

is a disjuncture in the ideal and the reality, given that many conservative Protestant women have entered the workforce, either through choice or necessity. Evangelical family "experts" such as James Dobson preach the message of the glories of motherhood and a woman's special role. The fall of housewives from their well-deserved pedestal is blamed on radical feminists (Balmer, 1994:55). Such idolization comes at a price. As Karen McCarthy Brown puts it, "Women can be idolized only when their sphere of activity is carefully contained and their power scrupulously monitored" (1994:181). In reaction to the perceived threats of the modern world, conservative Protestant prescriptions for women's roles have become even narrower in recent decades, a position that Nancy Nason-Clark has described as "gender inerrancy," meaning that there is less room for compromise in the conceptualization of "appropriate" roles for men and women (1995a:112).

In what might be seen as a reaction to the liberating promises of feminism, there also seems to be a trend among evangelical leaders, and indeed among the male evangelical laity, to focus on better defining men's roles within Christian marriages.[1] This emphasis on the responsibility of men to their families is a '90s version of prescribed family roles within the evangelical tradition, which seems to hold out a promise to women akin to that of feminism: Partnership, not lordship, is the *real* meaning of Christian submission and headship. Men must stop abdicating their responsibilities to their wives and become equal participants in family life. Whether the message here is that men should re-enter family life as the dominant partner remains to be seen.

Although spiritual leadership is rhetorically the man's responsibility, it is clear that evangelical women, like many other groups of female religious participants, often find themselves as the spiritual gatekeepers of the home: "In conservative Christian households, men are exhorted to be the spiritual leader of the family, but women tend to be the keepers and bearers of daily religious practice" (Pevey et al., 1996). This is most commonly accomplished through ensuring that their children attend church

---

[1]The existence of the Promise Keepers movement is one piece of evidence that supports this premise. The Promise Keepers is an evangelical men's group, the central focus of which is the encouragement of men's responsibility for and within their families.

and Sunday school and generally model a Christian way of life. As part of their role as mothers, evangelical women transmit their worldview to the next generation.

Mothering

Conservative Protestant ideology presents the ideal Christian home as one in which the woman is a full-time mother and homemaker (Gesch, 1995). Despite their deviation from this ideal, and similar to other studies that have explored evangelical women (Gesch, 1995; Nason-Clark and Belanger, 1993; Beaman and Nason-Clark, 1997b), the women in this study juggle their home-related, work, and church responsibilities. Moreover, they place a high degree of priority on their mothering responsibilities.

Without a doubt, most evangelical women define their roles in relation to mothering and the attendant nurturing tasks that are seen to arise out of that role. While not all evangelical women are mothers, the majority see mothering as their pivotal role. For those whose children are grown, the role of grandmother is often seen as being central. Functions related to nurturing and caregiving include being there to meet the needs of family members, providing support and love, and being a listener, friend, and confidante. Practical aspects of nurturing include household chores, homemaking, and financial management. This finding is not unique to this study; for example, Susan Sered, in her study of female-dominated religions, found that women's religious lives are closely linked to their interpersonal involvement, particularly with family (1994). Randall Balmer argues that the identity of fundamentalist women is inextricably linked to their role as mothers (1994). It is clear that for evangelical women, mothering occupies a great deal of practical and emotional space.

If we return to Jane (moderate), Mary (traditionalist), and Beth (feminist), introduced in chapter 2, we can compare their approaches to mothering. For Mary, mothering can only be properly done when a woman is a full-time homemaker. The role of mother is directly linked to God's plan for women. For Jane, the role of mother necessarily consumes a great deal of her time, and with five children she can't think about an option other than full-time mothering. She links her desire to stay at home to her own upbringing and does not connect her decisions around mothering specifically to God's will for women generally. Beth, too, gives her role as mother central importance, but does not see any conflict between God's will for her and her desire to work in the paid labor force. She feels she can be a better mother, and be more fulfilled as a person, by having interests outside the home.

Although the role most clearly identified with is that of mother, evangelical women also see themselves as juggling multiple tasks, whether between the home and the paid labor force or within the home:

> Ok, I suppose, over the years it's been, ah, peacemaker, ah, chief cook and bottlewasher, ah, well, working in partnership in my husband and all that, though I'll give him credit for some things, um, probably, and it's probably only because I assume the role, not because it was expected of me as being the one that...bought the clothes and did the groceries, and because that was the role I assumed. (#88, age 50)

One of the interesting aspects to emerge in relation to roles is that mothering, and not the role of wife, is the primary role by which women identify themselves. For women who have no children, this role shifts to that of wife. The following woman, who has no children, defined her role in her family in relation to her husband:

> My most important role is, is a partner with my spouse. And partnership for me is um, not always fifty-fifty, sometimes it's twenty-seventy or ninety or eighty and it gives and takes. Um, my biggest role is that I am, I am there to work with him as his wife, as his partner versus someone who's just married to him, and my sole goal is to be his wife. There's more to it, there's more of a partnership. (#62, age 32)

As the primary caregivers and nurturers, evangelical women see themselves as the center of the home. This is often described as "setting the tone" or mood of the family. In a very real sense, evangelical women see their families' well-being as contingent on their own actions and attitudes. Setting the tone is viewed as an important function that has the power to affect all the other family members:

> Kind of like a hub of a wheel, perhaps, if I dare take that spot, um...we decided, before...well, before we got married, we had decided, I had wanted it as much as my

husband, because we had both grown up with moms at home, and ah, my husband has a very hectic schedule…kids as they come, it was easy with one, two it's not so bad, but when you have three as we do, and I suppose anybody with any more, there's gotta be a lot more teamwork, and I'm a very organized person, and that often is the factor that keeps things running smoothly, and if I'm not well, or if I'm away, which is very seldom, you see how that's…um…can cause a…this is too strong a word, but turmoil, but it really allows my husband to have the freedom that he has, he's very committed to the family as well, but because of the job that he has, there's things that are unexpected at times, demands on his time that he can't control necessarily. (#55, age 33)

This theme of "setting the tone" also emerged in other research with evangelical women (Beaman and Nason-Clark, 1997b). Women see their roles in the home as central to the success of the family, both on a daily basis and in the long-term. Their recognition of their personal role is an important indicator of women's perceptions of their own agency in the context of the patriarchal structure of the church and the hierarchical "ideal" for Christian families.

While they define themselves primarily in terms of their mothering roles, it is unclear whether this is a result of the fact that they are immersed in a church culture that emphasizes the importance of women as mothers and nurturers or whether the centrality of the mothering role is experientially based. Does the emphasis on, and indeed glorification of, mothering minimize women's agency both within their own lives and in relation to social issues? Certainly, within their own families they perceive themselves to be partners, organizers, and even controllers.

The Evangelical Wife

Although evangelical women are first and foremost mothers, they also see their partnerships with their husbands as important anchors in meeting the challenges of day-to-day life. For evangelicals, the touchstone for marital relations is the notion that the husband is the head of the household, and the wife has a duty to submit to the husband. Wives are called to submit to their husbands in the Bible. Ephesians 5:22–25 (KJV) states:

> Wives, submit yourselves unto your own husbands, as unto the Lord. For the husband is the head of the wife, even as Christ is the head of the church: and he is the saviour of the body. Therefore as the church is subject unto Christ, so let the wives be to their own husbands in every thing. Husbands, love your wives, even as Christ also loved the church, and gave himself for it.

Although the Bible does make reference to submission, the interpretation of its meaning is man-made and developed in a particular social context. The patriarchal cultural context that existed at the time of the writing of this passage likely dictated the injunction to submit (Schüssler Fiorenza, 1992, 1994); Torjesen, 1995).

Women were associated with the "inferior" body, while men were linked to the "superior" mind. Such a mind/body duality facilitated the development of a hierarchy of marital relations between men and women, which saw women as the subordinate party in the relationship. As such, women needed to be protected and controlled, which included the right, indeed obligation, of husbands to chastise their wives (Bussert, 1986:9–11). Men were seen as being superior and different.

Although the rhetoric of submission has survived, we must be cautious about taking it at face value. It is important to undertake a careful examination of the interpretation of submission in day-to-day life. As a part of this study, I conducted a content analysis of thirty-eight issues of one evangelical publication. While there was no specific mention of submission in those issues, there was a debate over roles for men and women in the public sphere. Compare, for example, the following statements:

> The Church, on the basis of the total context of Scripture, believes that a woman is fully equal to man in terms of her right (as directed by the Holy Spirit and authorized by the Church) to teach, preach, lead or govern (including supervisory roles and board memberships), lead worship or serve in any other office or ministry of the Church. (Leading church official, March 1992)

> While this principle of male leadership is repulsive to our society today, it is nevertheless God's plan…It is true that a few women performed varying functions in the Old

Testament and in the early Christian church. This fact alone does not establish *Christian principle*. When Christ chose people to be His disciples and to lead the church after He ascended, He chose men. If He had wanted to set up women in leadership He could have done so. (Letter in the Reader's Forum August, 1992)

Like the stories of the evangelical women I talked to, the publication reflected a model of partnership for men and women in the family. The God-language in this periodical was exclusively male, and the vast majority of authority positions reflected in its pages were male. Two-thirds of the authors were male as well.

Submission is not interpreted monolithically by evangelical Christians. Traditionalists think about its meaning differently than do feminists. In the traditional view, submission reflects a God-ordained "natural" hierarchy in which men are the leaders and women the subordinates. Beverly LaHaye is a well-known evangelical speaker who is representative of the traditionalist approach to submission:

The woman who is truly Spirit-filled will want to be totally submissive to her husband. Regardless of what the current trend towards "Women's Lib" advocates, anything which departs from God's design for women is not right. Submission does not mean that she is owned and operated by her husband but that he is the "head" or "manager." A manager knows how to develop and use the gifts in others. This is what God intended the husband to do for the wife. He helps her develop to her greatest potential. He keeps track of the overall picture but puts her in charge of areas where she functions well. This is a truly liberated woman. Submission is God's design for women. (1976:71)

Needless to say, this hierarchical portrayal of male-female relations has attracted much criticism from secular feminists. However, at least in this study, traditionalists represent only a small proportion of evangelical women. It is therefore important to examine the spectrum of evangelical interpretations of submission.

For example, evangelical feminists such as Letha Scanzoni and Nancy Hardesty argue that we must see Paul's call to submit as being inextricably linked to the cultural context in which it was written. They further point out that Christianity is not unique in its call for women's submission (1974:99). Evangelical feminists argue that submission is mutual, that there is no hierarchy in Christian relations between husbands and wives, only partnership. In this view, men and women are equal (see Scanzoni and Hardesty, 1974; Dorothy Pape, 1976; and Faith Martin, 1988). Among this group of evangelicals, there is a recognition that submission is often misinterpreted:

> The picture of Christian marriage usually given is one of an autocrat lording over a docile child-wife who has no mind of her own, no interests but those of her husband and children, and little inclination toward personal growth. It is dangerous teaching and can only work against the Christian principles of unselfishness, love, and striving toward Christian maturity—principles that God asks of all believers, whether male or female. (Scanzoni and Hardesty, 1974:102).

As we have already seen in previous chapters, evangelical women identify service as one of the hallmarks of their faith; the women I talked to did not see submission as an essential component of their commitment to God. Indeed, for those women who have children, it is the mothering role they emphasize, not their relationship with their husbands. Evangelical women do prioritize service, but this does not diminish their agency in their homes or in their relationships in church and community.

Wilson and Musick (1995) suggest that conservative Protestant women are less autonomous than other groups of women within their marriages. However, in examining everyday practices of women's paternalistic rhetoric of submission, the picture becomes more complex. Researchers like Judith Stacey have found that women are active agents who work as partners within their families.

> Though evangelicals often describe the ideal marriage as one of masculine "headship" and feminine submission, it is doubtful how much they carry this into practice. Judith Stacey has concluded that these marriages are in fact a "patriarchy of the last gasp," supporting her observation that the use of hierarchical language often masks the relative lack of rigid structure in most successful evangelical marriages. (Bendroth, 1993)

Similarly, Nancy Ammerman reports that fundamentalist women negotiate and shape their roles in their families (1987).

In translating organizational rhetoric into practice, evangelical women speak in terms of "partnership" when they talk about their relationships with their husbands. In its practice, mutuality characterizes submission. Evangelical women speak of love, respect, working together, compromise, putting the other person first, and making decisions jointly. This evangelical Christian woman discusses her views on submission:

> I think the Bible teaches submission to each other, I think we're to submit to each other. For one, for the wife, or the husband, to be never willing to submit would mean, you know, it's bound to end in conflict, if a husband loves his wife as the Bible teaches, as God loved the church, there'd be, there would be no problems with submission because he would want everything for her that would, that would please her and help her, and there would be no domineering and, and power struggles, but I think there are situations when financial decisions should be set down and, and talked over, or problems in the house to be, if they can't come to an agreement, somebody has to make the final decision in any business or anything, someone has to make the final decision, and perhaps that's the time for, I don't know which one, I guess maybe, the head of the home.
>
> [Interviewer: And is that always the husband or sometimes?]
>
> Not necessarily. I think it depends on the one that has the most knowledge on the topic. (#78, age 57)

Interestingly, while women talk about equality and partnership in their relationships, and indeed in their descriptions of the decision-making process—and my occasional observations of their interactions with their husbands would certainly support an egalitarian model—many evangelical women also acknowledge the more hierarchical teachings of the church in relation to submission. The following statement was made by a woman who was married to a pastor. It represents the complexity of women's understandings of submission:

> Well, I don't think of it as a doormat, but I think of it as, well, we sit down and we discuss things together, and then we talk it over, and the final decision is made, and I accept, that type thing. It's not my husband standing there and

saying you do that, then I just do it. It's not that. It's usually he asks if I mind or if I could do something, then yeah…sure, or no, I don't think I can right now! Submission goes hand in hand with the love a husband has for his wife, and there's a mutual respect there. This is in the ideal situation, and a lot of times the submission scripture is taken right out of context, and they forget the rest of it. It's "wives submit to your husbands," and so wives hate the verse, and I can understand that because you know, you get some kind of a chauvinist guy who's saying wha wha wha, you know, and yeah, we'd like to smack him too! There'd probably be husband abuse in that type! But no, if you read your Bible, before it says anything about the wives being submissive it says husbands are to love their wives as Christ loved the church. And that's a pretty tall order, but if you realize, if a man loved his wife that much he wouldn't do anything to hurt her and it would be pretty easy to love and respect a man that did that. (#7, age 41)

Traditionalists interpret submission in terms of obedience to one's husband. Yet even this appears to be negotiated, and the woman is not the docile doormat one might at first assume. For traditionalists, submission involves love, respect, and commitment to caring for children.

The complexities and contradictions involved in the interpretation of submission are illustrated by the following comments:

Oftentimes you'll hear Ephesians 5:22 quoted, it says that wives submit to your husbands; Ephesians 5:21 says submit to one another, and I look at the fact that our wedding had that verse, because the whole idea, I've never had a problem with submission, because my husband and I look at it as a team. The office that I worked for before I got married, I probably did the same percentage of work in that office as I do in the home. It seems like 90 percent, but I certainly wasn't the president or even a branch manager, and I did the most miserable work, which is the same way at home, but we needed somebody at the top, to maintain, um, that had his arms in more places maybe, that, um, if there was a major decision, I mean we talk about the fifty-fifty, but when it comes down to a major decision, and you're like this [at a standstill], what do we do, and we can reason things out as much as possible, and be still in doubt with yes and no, and there's got to be somebody that's going to say, okay, well, I've got the last word, and God in scripture tells us it's the man. But, if the man is loving us as Christ loved the church, he's not doing it with the intention of pushing us into the ground and controlling us either, and I…so I think of submission it's looking for the best in another, I guess I've never really verbalized it, kind of thing, I submit to my children every day, but their schedules, and their needs as younger people in this world, ah, but yet they don't control me. It's looking out for their best interests, looking out for my family's best interests by staying home, um. It's a "want to" attitude, not a "have to" attitude. (#55, age 33)

Clearly, even moderate or traditional understandings of submission includes a notion of mutuality, in that the husband is to perform his "end of the bargain" as well. Over and over again I heard "We are not doormats" in response to probing about the issue of submission and how it plays out in the participants' everyday lives.

For many women, submission also means that the husband is the "head" of the household, although that headship is often viewed as a power of last resort when an impasse has been reached in the process of making a decision. Women point out that this final authority is exercised rather infrequently, if ever, within their marriages. While willing to subscribe to submission, women are sometimes defensive about its meaning in their lives in relation to their own autonomy.

I would like to think that my husband has the leadership role. I don't want it. I have enough responsibility just looking after the kids and a part-time job, and you know, there are very few decisions that are not made with both of us, but when it comes to actual leadership I have no problem with letting him be the leader in my home. (#1)

In practice, submission clearly does not eliminate the possibility of their own agency within their relationships with their husbands.

Evangelical feminists are far less likely to accept submission as a part of their marital relationships, no matter how it is interpreted. The following woman has developed a justification for rejecting submission that is similar to that argued by some Christian feminist theologians[2]:

> I have a hard time with that! [she laughs] I don't really believe that women should be in submission to men. Now whether I'm nonscriptural or not, I just cannot…I believe that when…it was about women being submissive to men in the Bible, that it was more of a cultural thing of the times, I don't believe that God wants us to be in submission to men. I think we were both created as humans and that neither one of us is to be in submission to another. And I think a lot of things, the way women feel that they have to act towards men, and that men have this position over them…when the Bible was interpreted it was so much of the…of the times. So much of that was brought into the scriptures, and it can't help not being because the people that wrote the scriptures…were living in these times, and this is what they knew and it was so acceptable, and it was the norm. And people imply that you have to be like that today, and I just don't believe that we do. (#48, age 32)

Evangelical women express frustration about the misuse of submission in relation to scriptural misinterpretation. They are also critical of clergy who interpret submission contrary to their own understandings, especially if the mutuality of submission is ignored or downplayed. This forty-five-year-old feminist expressed frustration about the ways in which the Bible has been used to perpetuate the subordinate status of women:

> Oh, man! I think that submission is…drastically misunderstood and especially in the church, the passages where submission have been very misunderstood. In fact, I took a course at the divinity school on women in the biblical record, and we looked at a lot of the so-called difficult passages and did some very good exegesis on them, and they, not only have, have they been misunderstood, they've been mistranslated, words have been mistranslated and you know, the word for, there's one word that can be very loosely translated as "do this quietly" or "be quiet about

---

[2]See, for example, Schüssler Fiorenza (1985, 1992), Ruether (1983b).

it," or "be silent," you know, there are very strong differences there, and often when it's done, ah, translated in relationship to women, it's be silent, be quiet, do not say anything, rather than be quiet or um, in, in, in the sense of not being noisy. (#64, age 45)

Evangelical women define submission in a variety of ways and actualize their beliefs to reflect these multiple interpretations. The majority of conservative Protestant women interpret submission not on the "radical" edges of traditionalism or feminism, but in a middle-ground manner. This moderate interpretation emphasizes equality, mutuality, and partnership in their marital relations. Submission to each other is central to this moderate approach. R. Marie Griffith reports similar findings in her research with Women Aglow. She highlights the importance of taking women's accounts of submission seriously:

> While many outsiders might readily assume that conservative Christian women such as those who belong to Aglow are merely participating in their own victimization, internalizing patriarchal ideas about female submission that confirm and increase their sense of personal inferiority, the women themselves claim that the doctrine of submission leads both to freedom and to transformation, as God rewards His obedient daughters by healing their sorrows and easing their pain. Thus interpreted, the doctrine of submission becomes a means of having power over bad situations, including circumstances over which they otherwise may have no control. (1997:172)

There is some concern that the headship model emphasized within evangelical Christian ideology leaves women especially powerless economically (Heggen, 1993:91). By emphasizing the home-based functions of nurturing and caretaking as the roles for which women are best suited, women are likely to become isolated and increasingly dependent on their husbands (Bussert, 1986:26). Certainly this may happen in some instances, but these must be balanced with the reality that many evangelical women participate in the paid labor force. In addition, evangelical women are frequently not only wage earners, but the family financial managers as well.

During the course of the ninety-four interviews and contact with nearly two hundred evangelical women through focus group research, I became increasingly aware of the degree to which evangelical women exercise agency in their relationships with their families, their churches, and their communities. They do not see themselves as powerless servants who wait for their husbands to come home and tell them what to do. Rather, evangelical women have interpreted submission so as to preserve and enhance their own agency. They emphasize partnership and mutuality in their relationships with their husbands, not the familial patriarchy that seems to the outsider to be explicit in the call to submit.

As a feminist who does not subscribe to an evangelical worldview, I have been fascinated, and to be honest sometimes repulsed, by the idea that a woman would describe her partner as her "head." But understanding submission simply as a patriarchal prescription that works to "keep women in their place" does not capture the complexity of the transition of submission from ideology to practice. For these evangelical women, who are called to subscribe to the doctrine of submission, it is a rhetoric that they reshape to meet their needs as active and equal participants in their own marital relationships.[3]

God, Family, and Work

The family has been identified as one of three institutions (the others being church and school) of central importance to the preservation and transmission of Christian beliefs and values (Ammerman, 1987; Rose, 1993). James Davison Hunter argues that family is one area of their lives in which evangelicals are least likely to compromise (1987b; 1991). The family, to conservative Protestant Christians, is "both the basic social unit of any community and the principal source of nurture and support for members of the community, especially its children; it is critical that the family be permanent and stable" (Leehan, 1989:86). The ideal Christian family is often presented as one in which the male is the leader, who works outside the home as the "breadwinner"; the female stays at home full-time to care for children and makes her family her top priority. Paid work for the wife is acceptable

---

[3]Mine is not the only research to explore the realities of the practice of submission. Pevey has found that the fundamentalist women she studied redefined submission "in a manner that enables them to maintain a sense of personal autonomy" (Pevey et al., 1996:187).

only if she can still make the care of her family her first priority (Heggen, 1993:86).[4] Evangelical Christians link the role of women as mothers and men as breadwinners specifically to God's plan for Christian family living. This woman reflects a traditionalist approach to women and the paid labor force:

> Probably there's so much unemployment and all that today I guess because of, um, a lot of women out taking, not taking jobs, just the difference in the workforces. Um, probably I have a problem, um, with someone who is unemployed, a man who is unemployed and can't take care of a family and a job that's, has physical labor, um, that a woman is in to prove that she can do. You know, I believe that um, the Lord gave us certain abilities and talents and to use those as they are used, we can do great and mighty things in this country. Um, we can have children at home being nurtured, I mean I'm talking idealistic here, um, being nurtured and brought up and given values and morals. Um, we wouldn't have the problems we do in the school system. There would be someone home after school with these children and um, …it's started off with so, with such great hope and it's led into something, you know…who do you blame for men who abuse their wife? You know, is it because there wasn't the support, the nurturing in that when they were brought up? And I have to tell you that no, there wasn't. Because the Bible tells us that, um, we bring our children up in the way they are, that they won't, they won't go that way. And again I'm speaking idealistically. (#56)

To this woman, women's and men's roles are clearly differentiated, and it is when either strays from the boundaries of those roles that "trouble" begins.

How do workforce participation and religious participation link together? Lyn Gesch has done a careful analysis of labor force participation and women's religiosity. She has found that rates of public participation differ little between full-time–employed women and full-time homemakers (1995:130). However, she does

---

[4]Heggen argues that this is actually not a biblical model, but is more a reflection of industrialization and urbanization, which has seen the division of the family's daily life into separate spheres (Heggen, 1993:86).

link decreased private religious behavior, such as prayer and Bible reading, to workforce participation. She also links feminist orientation to lower church attendance and activity.

The actual translation of ideology into practice is not always clear. There was no significant difference between feminists, traditionalists, and moderates in relation to workforce participation, church-related activities, and church attendance among the women who participated in this study. The differences, therefore, were in rhetoric and tone, rather than in practice. The following two statements reflect the process by which two women reached decisions related to participation in the paid labor force:

> In the sense that when we got married, it was a decision that there would be some compromise, that I wasn't just going into this and expecting [my husband] to live with whatever career decisions I made, um…decisions as to where we live and what we do with our time would be something that we would decide together, with our mutual goals and interests in mind. It wasn't just "I'm in this for as long as you will let me do what I want." And also from the perspective that, even though I do love the career that I started— I'm a teacher— that when children came along that one of us had to be able to be home with them, the idea of sacrifice…that it is not just a commitment that ends if feelings change, there's more…it's more than just a relationship for as long as it's satisfying, it feels good, sort of thing. That it's longer than that, it's a commitment for life, where I sense from people in the world the relationship is there as long as it satisfies you, and if doesn't…if it's not satisfying then it's okay just to end the relationship, which is not something that I believe is right. (#14, age 32)

And:

> My husband and I felt that I should be at home was also based on our, you know, what the Bible teaches the role for a woman to be. And, ah, just as the responsibilities that are expected as a mother. And also I think that sometimes when you go out to work that perhaps you feel more independent and maybe you have a different attitude towards your husband, you don't want to be as [pause] maybe as submissive. And I think the Bible teaches us as

Christian women that we should be submissive to our husbands. And I think why I say that is since I have gone out to work and now I'm in a different situation where I am living by myself most of the week, you do have a tendency to be more independent and maybe not be as, quite as submissive as you should be to your husband. You know, so you do have to, you know, I think the Lord kind of has to, ah, bring you to a point where you have to realize, "Okay, now your husband is back in the home again and ah, you know. You have to kind of sit back and, and be a bit more submissive." (#27, age 46)

What becomes clear from their discussions of family, work, and marriage is that it is difficult to separate women's lives into neat conceptual packages. The traditionalist quoted above is quite capable of living on her own during the week. Indeed, she described a pleasant life of part-time paid labor, baking, reading, and socializing with friends. She links going to work with independence, connecting it to lack of submission. How, exactly, she becomes more submissive when her husband returns at the end of each week was not entirely clear. It seemed that her "submission" was similar to the accommodation anyone would make when resuming the sharing of a household with another person. However, this woman's interpretation of that process is firmly rooted in her Christian worldview.

Marriage and Divorce

Central to the creation and maintenance of the ideal Christian family is the institution of marriage. Marriage is not simply a contract, but a covenant before God, which includes a lifelong commitment and promise of fidelity. To conservative Protestant Christians, God is an ever-present partner in the marital relationship. How do evangelical women think about marriage? Overwhelmingly they see it as a commitment for life. Non-Christians are seen as being likely to give up on their marriages too soon, not taking their vows seriously. For evangelical women, the preservation of the family is an important, if not sacred, task. From their perspective, it is part of their mission to manage tension and to act as a "peacekeeper," a task that they see as being specifically rooted in their Christian commitment.

Relationship preservation also involves a particular attitude or approach, which includes moral boundaries and sacrifice for the good of the family. This woman expresses her views about Christian marriage in this way:

> To clarify, I don't know, nowadays, if …it can even differ from other Christians…because it's sad to say, we've bought into a lot of secular opinion, and that we serve ourselves. The Bible teaches us that we serve others, and I think as the children come and I've had to give up things that I like to do, I've had to do it with a servant attitude, and it's a constant thing…even that the longer I am at home, in some respects it doesn't necessarily get easier, it's just a commitment that I know is there and so you have to look at the long-term results, and that isn't how I feel today, and how the children possibly feel, um, you can't always see results with children today, and so you don't say well, gee, I feel miserable, I've got, um…when my third one was born, was not four yet, and so at that point in time if I based what I was doing on how physically I felt and how emotionally I felt, I would have been out the door, but that's not what you base it on. I think oftentimes, other Christians or non-Christians base it on their self-esteem and what makes you feel good at the moment. And the moment I don't think is a good judge of what you do. (#55, age 33)[5]

And:

> Probably the first thing that would come to my mind in response to that [question about marriage] would be my commitment to it is…unquestioned. Like, when I think of walking out of my marriage, like those thoughts…I don't entertain those thoughts at all. And that's because of my…that value that I put on the vows that I made, and the scriptures that support those vows. And therefore its not…it doesn't seem to loom over me as a possibility or a threat…or…an option. Therefore, when things go wrong and things are a problem and it's been a hard day, that's not where I would find release for my frustrations. By

---

[5]There are some secular researchers who make similar points about the "decline" of marriage. See, for example, Romaniuc (1994:222).

> saying, okay, you know, this isn't working, I think I'll just
> pack and go…that to me seems not working towards it at
> all, and I'm committed to my vows, I'm committed to my
> husband, I'm committed to my kids, and I wouldn't want
> to let any of those things down just because I decide that
> it's too much effort to me. (#2, age 40)

As this woman's comments indicate, Christian prescriptions for marriage are seen not as prohibitive or restrictive, but rather as empowering, in the sense that she knows that she can count on them as standards.

The need to make others happy, to put the needs of one's family first, and to have a servant attitude are seen as being distinctive features of Christian marriages. Yet the emphasis on "others first" does not mean that evangelical women are doormats for their families; as we have already seen, evangelical women see themselves as setting the tone for daily family living. From the quotation above we again get the sense that the guidelines and ideals that are a part of the conservative Protestant worldview are not seen as restrictive, but rather provide a course along which one can steer a steady path in an unstable and uncertain world.

Not only is marriage "for life," but it is inextricably linked to spirituality. Marriage to these women is God-instituted, and scripturally prescribed and benefits from God's guidance. Some women described how God brought them together with their husbands as part of God's plan.

> I feel that God has ordained marriage, that he has created,
> he has designed us to be most fulfilled when we are
> husband and wife, committed until death do us part. And
> I don't think that non-Christians feel that same commit-
> ment,…they may say, oh, yes, I definitely want to stay with
> my spouse, but as far as feeling that God has kind of laid
> his hands on their marriage, and the blessing in that way,
> they would have no understanding of that. And I firmly
> believe the circumstances in which [my husband] and I
> came together were such that we really feel that God
> brought us together…so I know that that is different than
> in what some non-Christians would think. (#49, age 39)

> I think in a Christian marriage God joins you together.
> There is a direct…linking of His blessing within the couple.
> And [my husband] and I have really experienced that. I

was a non-Christian when I met him, so it was all the more, when I became a Christian, it was all the more reason that this was definitely God's will and His union for us. And in some ways we were...we were marrying out of that sense of obedience in knowing that God was joining us together. We loved each other, but there was more to it. And I think as a non-Christian oftentimes you get caught up in the pageantry of weddings, the hoopla, the dress, and the dinners, and, and walking down the aisle. For me it was "I'm going to marry someone that I'm going to spend the rest of my life with, and this is exciting." I didn't care whether my dress was long or short or white or pink or blue. So I think it does make a huge difference in the sense that God is there within a Christian marriage and in the secular world is just not. (#62)

To evangelical women, God is the spiritual head of the family, ever present and accessible in times of trouble.

Through their reflections on marriage, and their descriptions of how they see their marriages as different from those who do not subscribe to a Christian worldview, we can see that evangelical women perceive themselves to be more committed to their marriages and to the preservation of the family. While commitment is a somewhat vague concept that is difficult to quantify (in fact, research suggests that the divorce rate among Christians is almost as high as the rate among non-Christians), participants did articulate the differences more clearly in relation to the presence of God and his support. Evangelical women described praying with their husbands for solutions to family problems, as well as a general sense of well-being brought about by a shared commitment to "doing the work of the Lord" together.

Their perceptions of non-Christian marriages also reflect what evangelical women consider to be distinctive boundaries between themselves and the secular world. Indeed, in some cases I felt that they were so desirous to distinguish their marriages as different that the characterization of non-Christian marriages as being based on selfish self-indulgence was, to say the least, an exaggeration. Like those in the secular world who interpret the dynamics of Christian marriages to mean that Christian women are submissive servants who live life with no thoughts of their own, Christian women sometimes portrayed non-Christian relationships as temporary arrangements that fall apart after the first spat about the toothpaste tube.

Divorce and the Christian Image

Certainly there is a pervasive rhetoric within evangelical Christianity that marriage is for life. However, the vast majority of the women who participated in this study believed that there are situations, primarily those involving abuse or adultery, when separation or divorce is acceptable, although their standards are different when a Christian family is involved. Conservative Protestant Christians are often portrayed as condemning divorce except in narrowly, biblically prescribed situations.

Despite what women see as clear biblical support for adultery as justification for ending a marriage, most women identified abuse, and not adultery, as the most powerful justification for separation and divorce. Abuse was often broadly defined:

> I don't think we're ever called to take abuse, and I think that takes in more than just physical abuse. I think if you are living constantly under mental abuse, if you are verbally abused, I don't believe that God called us to be destroyed in a relationship. (#70, age 52)

While adultery was seen as justification for marriage termination, many women added that it did not mean that there should be no effort made to repair the marriage relationship when one of the partners had committed adultery. The idea of reconciliation in the case of any marriage difficulty, though not often articulated as such, was pervasive among these women.

> I don't know quite how to put that. Personally, divorce is something that I don't look upon it with…positive eyes. And I think…if there is a situation, life threatening, that you can't go back into, and…the partner wants out, and wants a divorce, you pretty much have to grant it. The world today, well it's just like Moses said for the hardening of your heart the divorce, the bill of divorce was written. And that's what it is—it's the hardening of the heart towards each other. But it is not something that I think that, that should be jumped at lightly, if at all. Everything should be, oh, everything should be tried first before that

comes to that unless there is a real awful hatred towards one another, you know. (#9, age 60)

Evangelical women also recognize that there are times when a couple simply cannot reconcile or make a marriage work. However, they are careful to emphasize that they do not have a "lax" attitude toward marriage termination and that everything should be done to salvage a marriage before the decision to separate is made.

> Well, it has to be more than an…unhappy relationship you can work out. I mean, there are times when I'm unhappy, I mean there are times when everyone is unhappy in their situation, but I mean, you work through that. It has to be a lot more than just being, because you are not personally satisfied. I'm not saying because you are not personally satisfied then you should go on. That's not what I'm saying at all. There is a much, much deeper sense of commitment than that. But it is to the point where you, like one person is just not going to change and he's just completely destroying your life and there is no end, all you see is a black tunnel without ever a light. Whenever I'm in an unhappy situation I always see that…really two weeks down the road things will be fine again. But when I'm in that sort of situation I think I couldn't live like this if there was never an end, if it was always like this. (#1, age 47)

There is a tendency, especially in relation to Christian families, to think in terms of keeping the family together at all costs. Perhaps this can be understood not only in the context of the emphasis on forgiveness within the Christian worldview, but also in relation to the belief that with God's support, reconciliation and healing are both possible and desirable.

Although divorce is generally viewed as being undesirable, it takes on a special poignancy when a Christian couple is involved. Evangelical women admit that they hold Christian couples to a different standard. They talk about their personal feelings of sadness and disappointment when a Christian marriage "comes to that," especially given the resources available to Christians such as prayer and the Bible. It is difficult to accept that a Christian family has come to that point, especially since Christians have resources not available to non-Christians.

Um, well, sometimes, it just happened recently in our church, and I felt badly, that God couldn't pull them together, you know…they both seemed to love the Lord, and I said, gee, isn't it too bad that they couldn't pray their way through it. And we…have been lifting up in prayer as a church, and I do think, I see them together sometimes, I don't know whether it's for the children's sake or what, I mean, it doesn't matter, I'm glad if I see them together, I know that there is something good there. At least they're trying, for the children's sake. (#59, age 46)

High expectations mean that evangelicals have a difficult time accepting that a "truly" Christian couple could come to the point of divorce:

Well, because they have, if they are truly Christian, and lots of people will tell you they are Christian, they mean they are good people, by a Christian I mean someone who is praying, who is seeking God's leading, who knows that there's a spirit of God that will enable them to do things they can't do on their own, that level of Christian, I think it's totally different. I think it's a power beyond your own, and if there's willingness on both parts, I think in most cases those couples can be reconciled, if they are both willing to and they are both relying on God and His power, you just have a dynamic that's not available, you can't ask non-Christians to be able to do that because it's beyond themselves. (#70, age 52)

And:

[S]ometimes when another couple who call themselves Christian does this, then yeah, I think that I would tend to think, well, did you really mean the vows, and I'd probably look at them maybe a little more judgmentally, and that's just a personal thing, not necessarily a good thing, but…it's a personal thing that I might look at them more critically than I would someone else, and think—you had God on your side, you know, this should have worked. (#49, age 39)

There is the feeling that Christian couples "knew what they were getting into" when they got married, meaning that there is an expectation of commitment within the faith community, which exacts a higher level of commitment than what is expected in the secular world. It is clear that in the context of a Christian marriage, reconciliation is a goal to strive for. When a Christian marriage ends, evangelical women feel sad, let down, shocked, and hurt. There is a perception that Christian couples have more resources to help them through hard times. The presence and strength of God is seen as a distinguishing factor in Christian marriages; divorce is evidence that a couple has not relied on God to help them through hard times and that the Bible has been ignored as a standard for family living.

Although Christians are seen to have unique resources and a unique commitment, they are also recognized as having human failings. "Bad backgrounds" and the lack of Christian commitment by one partner are seen as intervening variables in the path between Christian commitment and marriage for life. Though evangelicals believe in the transformative power of a Christian conversion, they also incorporate understandings of human agency in their explanations for failure to live up to Christian standards.

In ministering to their families, evangelical women negotiate the expectations of their husbands and children, the boundaries and role expectations set out by their churches, and a social context that contains multiple messages about mothering and the role of women in the paid labor force. The ordering of this complex picture begins with their Christian worldview.

5

Mothering the Congregation

Well, in activity, my life and what I enjoy doing centers around my activities in the church. Those are my aims and goals...the things that I am involved in are what promotes that life. There's Monday night's Bible study and Tuesday night prayer group and Tuesday night there is usually guild or Women's Mission, and on Wednesday night there's choir, and Thursday afternoon there's, ah, youth group and stuff that I'm involved in plus the Sunday, which I'm the organist, the organist here. (#9)

One of the primary ways evangelical women live out their call to service is through their church-related activities. These include not only regularly scheduled meetings and events, but special commitments such as fund-raisers, guest speakers, musical events, and so on. One of the most difficult aspects of service to "measure" as a researcher are those everyday acts of kindness evangelical women perform: visits to friends in the hospital or sick at home, casseroles for their families, and prayers for their health. During the course of the fieldwork, I heard countless references to the needs of others and the ways they could be met. Women are particularly sensitive to the needs of other women within their churches, but they do respond to community needs as well.

The linking of women as mothers and their nurturing roles within church congregations is nothing new. Debra Kaufman's extensive analysis of Orthodox Jewish women reveals that women do not differentiate their familial and community caretaking roles, but see their mothering, in the broader sense, as integrally connected to their spiritual roles. There is a sense that women are inherently more spiritual, and thus are better equipped to nurture than men. Nurturing extends beyond the immediate family to the church and community.

Mothering has also been a central interest of feminist theory. Rooted in the biological and psychological divergences of women and emulating in many ways maternal feminism, the difference approach celebrates that which is characterized as uniquely female, including mothering. Theories that explore and honor women's differences based on mothering are rooted in maternal feminism. Maternal feminist Sara Ruddick identifies a unity of reflection, emotion, and judgment, which she calls "maternal thinking" (Ruddick, 1984:214). She also argues that there exists a maternal practice that is directed toward preservation, growth, and understanding (1984:215). According to Ruddick, the work of mothering may have political implications because it "gives women distinctive motives for rejecting war and distinctive practice both in peacekeeping and in nonviolent forms of resistance to oppression" (Jaggar, 1990:248). As we have already seen, evangelical women define their roles in their families in relation to the importance of mothering, especially its attendant nurturing functions. Some women explicitly mentioned peace-making, identifying it as part of God's intended role for women.

One difficulty with maternal feminism is that it focuses only on the mothering role for women. As a result, it may work against expanding the definition of that role and rather be used as evidence that mothering is the only appropriate role for women. While Ruddick explains some of the consequences of mothering, her theory does not explain why women are primarily responsible for child-rearing (Flax, 1990:47). This theory also bears striking similarity to the first-wave version of feminism, which saw women in a special role as protectors of morality.[1] Finally, not all women have the capacity or the desire to mother, nor are experiences of mothering necessarily as similar as Ruddick portrays them to be.

---

[1]Maroney argues that there are some critical distinctions between first- and second-wave maternal feminism in her article "Embracing Motherhood: New Feminist Theory" (1986).

These disadvantages can be loosely translated in the world of evangelical women: Not all women are mothers or are "naturally" nurturers. Women who are mothers may not see that role as their primary basis of identity. Further, by highlighting mothering, women are often ghettoized into caretaking roles that exclude them from positions of power. It is this last point that has been the focus of much of the criticism about evangelical women and their role in the church.

What is the nature of evangelical women's activities within their church organizations? How does their religious commitment manifest itself in their everyday lives? Recent research with Wesleyan women would suggest that one way to characterize evangelical women is as "jugglers for Jesus" (Nason-Clark and Belanger, 1993; Nason-Clark and Beaman-Hall, 1994; Beaman and Nason-Clark, 1997b). For both women who stay at home and those who are in the paid labor force, daily life is filled with juggling church responsibilities, home, tension management, and stress caused by too little time to accomplish everything they want to do. Of the 287 women surveyed for the Wesleyan Woman project, 55 percent held at least two volunteer positions in the church (Nason-Clark and Beaman-Hall, 1994:2).

While more than half of the women in this study had at least two church-related responsibilities (and nearly one in five of the participants had between four and six church-related responsibilities), by far the most frequently mentioned responsibilities were related to childcare or nurturing, such as nursery duty, teaching children's Sunday school, or leading a youth group. Responsibilities also included choir membership or direction, playing the piano or organ for church services, leading women's groups, leading Bible studies, outreach ministries, and "other" responsibilities such as prayer chain membership.

Several women interviewed from one church were involved in an outreach ministry for young mothers. They met once a week, provided practical help to disadvantaged women, like providing groceries, and offered guest speakers on legal issues, budgeting, and so on. They also included a Bible study component in their morning of outreach, but that was not mandatory for the women who came. This form of outreach provided an important forum in which the women of the church were able to reach out to women in the community with whom they might otherwise never have contact. They saw this as an important part of their Christian commitment—service at a practical level, and the opportunity to witness both by example and through the Bible study.

Most of these responsibilities reflected a traditional division of labor within the church that sees women performing the caretaking and nurturing tasks and men holding positions of leadership, which determine the allocation of finances and the overall direction of the church (Nason-Clark, 1993). How can we make sense of the nature and extent of women's activities within the church? They certainly reflect women's mothering, caretaking role in their homes, but should they simply be interpreted as structurally imposed "choices" that aren't really choices at all? If we take the number of church-related responsibilities of evangelical women as a measure of commitment, we can clearly argue that they are active members of the thirty or so churches they represent. On more traditional measures of commitment, evangelical women score high.

While measures of attendance alone are poor indicators of religiosity (Bibby, 1987)[2], attendance does provide one piece of the commitment puzzle.[3] Thirty-nine percent of the women in this study attended church services once each week, 29 percent attended twice each week, and 16 percent attended three times each week. In other words, 80 percent of the women interviewed attended church at least once a week.[4] One of the negative aspects of their intensive church involvement is the risk of "burnout."

---

[2]As an example, one of the participants was a pastor who had recently completed her training. During her school years, when she attended church as part of her training, she did not participate in church-related groups on a regular basis and did not read church-related publications on a regular basis. Thus, even the variety of approaches used in this study to evaluate religiosity are inaccurate in that particular case.

[3]Yet, even attendance is not as easily measured as one might think; many churches have moved from a mid-week service to either a prayer meeting format or cell group format. Many of the women did not seem to consider participation in these groups as "attendance." In addition, some women considered attendance at church and attendance at Sunday school to be two separate "attendances," even though they were both on Sunday morning. Participation in the mid-week Bible study has thus been included as "involvement in church group" rather than attendance. Attendance at both Sunday school and the church service has been counted as only one "attendance."

[4]Other aspects of worldview reinforcement are reading materials, television, and Christian videos. More than 80 percent of the participants read church-related publications on a regular basis. Seventy-seven percent have favorite Christian authors and one-third watch Christian television programs on a regular basis. Forty percent named Christian videos that they had found inspirational. Many participants (63 percent) reported that at least 50 percent of their friends were Christian.

Some women find themselves withdrawing from church activities entirely, in an effort to regain a sense of order or to prioritize other responsibilities. It became evident, in talking to women, that it is important to consider the life cycle of church activity, which can vary significantly as a woman moves through various stages of life. When asked about the extent of her involvement in church activities, this woman replied:

> Well, at the moment I have downscaled my involvement in responsibilities at the church because I felt like I needed a lesser workload at the church for a while because with the boys and with how busy we are on that end. But I like to be fully involved at the church level and I have done a number of things. I have been on the board, taught Sunday school, clubhouse ministries for children, church typist, church secretary, social committee—if it's going on I like to be a part of it. I enjoy the church leadership end, but I found that I've had to cut back. (#2)

There are a couple of interesting observations to be drawn from this statement. First, there is a life cycle to church activity that means that life history data will provide a more accurate picture of the relationship between women and their faith communities. Second, like many women, this woman saw her activities as being about leadership. She does not make the distinction between the roles reserved for men and the leadership roles she has fulfilled. For some women, mothering their own children involves taking on increased responsibilities in the church, such as becoming youth leaders. In this way they mother their children and the congregation simultaneously.

Despite all of their activity and hard work, women are systematically excluded from positions of leadership like pastor or deacon. Only ten of the women I interviewed held such positions. But can we simply dismiss the leadership positions women *do* hold, such as choir director, Sunday school leader, or Bible study coordinator, as extensions of women's nurturing roles, which do not involve the exercise of any "real" power? It first depends on how we conceptualize and measure power. If we limit power to hierarchical notions that privilege the positions men have traditionally held, and if we think of power as being "held," we will inevitably conclude that women are indeed relatively powerless within church structure. If we conceptualize power as relational, and think about women's empowerment, the picture will be a bit different.

Brenda Brasher's (1997, 1998) research with two fundamentalist women's groups is particularly instructive in helping us to make sense of the structure-agency relationship and power. Brasher explores the spaces women create for themselves in the context of two traditionally organized, patriarchal, fundamentalist churches. She argues that while men use the presence of the "sacred wall of gender" to appropriate almost all congregational authority for themselves, women use "the presence of the sacred gender wall to rationalize the development of extensive ministry programs run exclusively for and managed solely by women" (1998:13). What is especially significant about Brasher's analysis is that she does not minimize the importance or nature of the power relations involved in the women-only space. Interestingly, Brasher mentions men's envy of women's experiences and space. Brasher's research also revealed that no women expressed interest in being involved in the male-dominated administrative positions. "Thus, to some men as well as many women the ministries women are generating on their side of the sacred gender wall are a highly desirable good, evidently to some even more desirable than what men were generating on their side of the divide" (1997:242). If religious participation is about spiritual fulfillment, women appear to have more opportunity to pursue it through their involvement in church women's groups.

Brasher's research should not be read as a negation of the need or desirability for women in administrative positions. However, it does draw out the rather narrow ways in which power has been conceptualized in analyses of women's roles in the church. By adopting a male-stream conceptualization of power, we set up a framework in which women's agency is necessarily discounted. By emphasizing the relational aspects of power, we can rethink women-only spaces as sources of women's empowerment. Such a reconceptualization is a delicate balance. Recognizing the importance of women-only spaces while at the same time opening the door for women's wider participation in all aspects of church life requires an acknowledgment of both hierarchical and relational aspects of power.

A strictly dualistic conceptualization of church leadership must be more closely examined. While the vast majority of evangelical clergy are male, women do have access to other powerful leadership positions, which are frequently minimized. Brasher talks about the authority, both ascribed and achieved, that comes with being the pastor's wife. Ignoring this power is a result of a very narrow conceptualization of power. Without a doubt, women have less access to administrative positions. Yet it is important to explore power and authority in a manner that moves beyond the surface of the formal hierarchy of the church. Although this study did not focus on pastors' wives, it included a number of women in that position. They clearly occupied a unique status in their church communities, one that was, as Brasher points out, both ascribed and achieved.

Like the women in Brasher's study, many of the evangelical women who participated in this study felt that they had enough to do and most had little interest in taking on the administrative positions in the church. The following fifty-five-year-old nurse supported the full participation of women in church administration, but based her support on a notion of women as being different from men:

> I think a woman should have a right to offices in the church …like our church has no female deaconesses, but…I feel we should—I think we should…because sometimes a woman's viewpoint differs from a man, but I think we need both viewpoints in the church. (#21)

Another aspect of the gendered division of labor in churches is that women sometimes buy into the rhetoric of limited leadership roles for women, thus resulting in their sanctioning women who do aspire to traditionally male-held leadership roles. One woman pastor reported that her ability to communicate with some female parishioners was limited:

> She's [a member of the congregation] very fundamentalist and doesn't believe women should be in ministry, so we have a barrier there. So it's kind of like Satan is using you, and so I'm not very credible. (#65)

Although it is important to support the administrative participation of women, a reexamination of the ways in which we conceptualize power is also necessary. Central to women's power within church organizations are church groups.

Church Groups

The vast majority of evangelical women are involved in one or more church groups, most often women-only groups. In addition to church attendance, half of the participants in this study were involved in one church group, and a further third were involved in two or three church groups. This did not include their church-related responsibilities mentioned earlier. Of the groups to which they belong, church women most frequently attend all-women groups such as Bible studies, fellowship groups, missions groups, and prayer groups. Nearly one-third of the participants are also involved in interdenominational groups outside their own church, such as Bible study groups and Christian fellowship groups. In one church the number of women who attended Bible study was so large that the group broke into smaller devotional groups where they could discuss issues more effectively.

> *We arrived at Riverside Baptist Church about 9:30 a.m., when women were still arriving in cars and walking up the street to this suburban church. When we went into the church we were greeted by Molly, one of the small-group leaders. She asked us if we would like to meet the pastor and we agreed, stopping by his office on our way to the large, finished basement of the church. About thirty women arrived, carrying Bibles in quilted or crocheted cozies, with children in tow. Cathy, the head of the women's ministry at Riverside, opened the meeting with a prayer, which included a thanks to God for our safe arrival and a plea for our safe return home. As we divided into four small groups, children were delivered to the nursery, and women gathered in groups of twos and threes to quickly share news about ailing parents and children's escapades, and to make social plans. The women gradually dispersed into the groups, located in separate rooms, and began different Bible studies. One group was made up of "older" women, one of young mothers, and two were "mixed." The conversations were interspersed with Bible verses, personal experiences, laughter, and sometimes tears as women shared their pain as well as their joys. When we came together briefly at the end of the morning, prayer requests were shared. Some women left quickly to make lunch for their families, others organized themselves to go out to lunch.*

Involvement in church-based groups is an important aspect of religious participation for women. Church groups provide a forum to which participants can bring their everyday problems and stresses. The process of talking about these problems creates a shared space and an affirmation of experiences with other Christians (Winston, 1994). Belonging to a group reinforces the boundaries that separate evangelical Christian women from the secular world. The group provides confirmation that this is a distinct group (Searl, 1994). Finally, church groups bring ordinary and everyday occurrences and actions under the "sacred canopy" of meaning. As Searl discovered in her study of an evangelical women's Bible study, "the meaning of the women's personal lives is enriched because the study helps them to see their small acts and ordinary activities in a divine context" (1994:118). Searl's research points to a key to interpreting the often extensive participation of evangelical women in church activities. Sunday school, choir, and so on are important ways in which women actualize their faith with what they see as one of the central components of that faith—service. Involvement in church activities functions as both a way to serve and a way to evangelize, albeit some of the "preaching" is to the "converted." Service allows evangelical women to model their Christian commitment to others.

As an expression of faith, service in the church is critical. To evangelical women, Jesus modeled service, and so too should they:

> As Christians, you consider what God has done for you, then, you know, sort of pass it on. You have an obligation to show the love of God to your fellow citizens. You're not much of a Christian if you are not doing that. I mean, Jesus didn't think of himself first, he didn't spend his time building mansions. (#52)

Indeed, some women see church service as an extension of family life. Service in the family necessarily involves a commitment to the activities of the church. Service in the group context includes spiritual pursuits such as prayer requests:

> I belong to a Wednesday morning Bible study group, and very often we bring our prayer concerns to this group. We may not bring a name, but we'll bring a situation, you know, we'll say, "I'd like to pray for my friend, who's having a problem with…"or if we have the permission of that person we may include a name. (#13)

Participation in women's groups also provides a space in which women can negotiate boundaries between their social context and the church (both organizationally and doctrinally).

As spaces that are run by women for women, evangelical women's groups provide a forum in which women come together to create a place for spiritual and personal growth, as well as the identification and meeting of the needs of women both within and outside of their faith community.

As a mechanism for outreach to the wider community, church women's groups are pivotal. I frequently heard reports of church women's groups making donations to transition houses or food banks. Even those women's groups formed to pray for the community combine "practical" outreach with prayer. Sometimes women become frustrated with the apathy of their congregations. One woman described the outreach program her woman's group has initiated. A component of it is the provision of bags of groceries to indigent women. The contents of those bags is provided by congregational donations:

> I find people are in general so engrossed in their own little world that they don't want to think beyond that or they're so busy being a success they don't have time for…like, I know the people have been good, they've been generous, but the food—there's seven hundred members here, like, those barrels should be overflowing. We have to keep reminding them and almost every week we have just enough to do those twenty-five bags. Just enough. The Lord provides just enough each week, but we could do so much more. (#77)

How does all of this translate in the everyday lives of evangelical women? Not only do they get up each Sunday morning and attend church and Sunday school, they may share Sunday dinner with Christian friends, their children may watch a Christian video in the afternoon, and then the family is off to church again for the Sunday evening service. The week may include Monday evening youth group for the children, Tuesday evening choir practice, Wednesday evening mid-week service or home cell group meeting, Thursday morning or evening "ladies" Bible study, Friday night and Saturday socializing with Christian friends, and then the week begins again. Though admittedly not all of the women who participated in this study have such church-centered lives, many of them do. For most women, an evangelical Christian worldview incorporates not only private daily devotional practices, but includes a lifestyle that involves a variety of activities in a pervasive evangelical culture.

At a structural level, the involvement by individual women translates into the smooth running of the day-to-day activities of evangelical churches. It is well known that women do the "grunge" work of churches. Women volunteers polish the brass, bake, serve and clean up for the church suppers, and transmit the Christian worldview to children within their families and through their church activities as Sunday school and youth group leaders (Nason-Clark, 1993). Women also mediate the relationship between churches and communities. In summary, they carry the faith within their families, their churches, and the communities in which they live, through both individual and group activities.

6

Secular Influences: Defining Feminism

Interviewer: Would you describe yourself as a feminist?

Participant: No, but I'm not a noodle either, nobody's going to walk over me.

Feminism is an issue that highlights the negotiating process between evangelical women, the church organization, and secular society. Yet the analysis is complicated because of the diverse nature of feminism and its complex relationship to mainstream society. The relationship between religion and secular culture is especially central to an examination of women's roles and experiences both in society and in the context of religious institutions for a variety of reasons. First, the historical relationship between religion and culture has implications for the subordination and oppression of women today. The impact of cultural traditions on religious forms cannot be underestimated. In the case of Christianity, for example, Schüssler Fiorenza (1985; see also Torjesen, 1995) argues that the equality message of the Jesus movement became quickly subsumed by the patriarchal culture in which it emerged and in which the subsequent Christian missionary movement (the beginnings of Christianity as a world religion) existed.[1]

_____
[1]See also Olive Banks (1986).

Second, religious messages in relation to the roles and responsibilities of women have been and continue to be shaped by cultural pressures. This is the central point of Betty DeBerg (1990) in her discussion of the first wave of fundamentalism in the United States at the turn of the century. DeBerg argues that the resurgence of fundamentalism was integrally connected to growing concern about the erosion of traditional gender roles. Schüssler Fiorenza points out that the intertwining of Christian faith and a sociocultural regime of subordination of women has meant that religion has been unable to adequately address violence against women (1994:xviii).

Third, not only has religion had a part, together with secular culture, in the reproduction of patriarchal culture, it has also provided the impetus for religious opposition to patriarchal structures in mainstream culture. One example of this is liberation theology, but the example of the countercultural aspects of the Jesus movement itself is often overlooked. The mixed messages regarding the role of religion in both the perpetuation of and opposition to patriarchal culture have resulted in a diversity of characterizations of religion as it relates to the lives of women.[2]

Religion and law have been described as the twin institutional pillars of patriarchy (Gorham, 1976:27). Cecelia Wallace describes the relationship between women's oppression and religion in this way:

> Ultimately all discrimination against women can be said to have its roots in the male interpretation of religion. The feminist revolution now in evidence everywhere in the world often fails to grasp that fact because today we have managed to divorce religion from everyday life in a manner which was never possible even fifty years ago.
>
> If women are really to destroy the basic prejudice against them they must deal analytically with this long religious tradition and eliminate it by producing women scholars in every religious field who can effectively argue against the male-oriented view of religion. (1976:127)

Women have themselves taken a variety of approaches in thinking about their own involvement in religion. As Naomi Goldenberg puts it, "Contemporary feminist critics of religion can

---

[2]For a brief discussion of the oppressive and liberating aspects of religion, see Anderson (1993).

be placed on a spectrum ranging from those who revise to those who revolt" (1979:13). Among the revisionists, many writers recognize that organized religion has perpetrated and facilitated the oppression of women (Gorham, 1976; Lerner 1986, 1993; Ruth Wallace, 1992; Daly, 1968, 1973, 1978). However, a number of explanatory models are employed to understand the nature and source of that oppression and possible strategies for gaining women's equality.

For example, Mary Daly, a "post-Christian" feminist, argues that "a woman's asking for equality between men and women in the church would be comparable to a black person's demanding equality in the Ku Klux Klan" (1968:6). For feminists such as Mary Daly and Naomi Goldenberg, women will only benefit from disassociation from the church. They see the church as being inherently patriarchal, so much so that it can only ever act in the interests of men. This approach has been criticized for excluding those women who have chosen to work within the boundaries of patriarchal culture. Another difficulty with Daly's argument is that her critique can be made about most social institutions (legal, political, economic, and kinship), leading to the question of women's involvement in any social institution. In contrast, some feminists have chosen to advocate change from within the boundaries of existing institutions.

Understanding religion as potentially both oppressive and liberating, these feminists have employed strategies such as biblical reinterpretation to enhance, include, and contextualize women's lives and experiences (Meyers, 1988; Ruether, 1983a, 1985; Schüssler Fiorenza, 1985; Miles, 1987). Through their work, either explicitly or implicitly, Christian feminists affirm the compatibility of feminism and Christianity (Christ, 1979; Langley, 1983; Scanzoni and Hardesty, 1974; Spencer, 1985; and Faith Martin, 1988). In other words, many of these scholars see the emancipation of women as being fully possible within the tenets of Christianity and do not see the equality message of feminism as contradictory to Christianity. Women should be equal within the church, within the family, and in society generally. Other writers emphasize the historical aspects of both women's oppression and empowerment within the Christian framework (Lerner, 1986; 1993). These writings are diverse,[3] ranging from

[3]For an illustration of this diversity, see Young (1992). Bineham argues that "Christian feminism, like the dominant tradition, is not a monolithic structure; various tensions exist among feminist theologians" (1993:521).

more conservative, apologetic approaches to radical reconstructions of biblical texts and religious ideologies. Moreover, Winter, Lummis, and Stokes (1994) have found that in everyday religious practice, women create their own woman-centered strategies within patriarchal religious settings, sometimes rejecting religious dogma altogether, an approach that they describe as "defecting in place." Within the evangelical context, however, we should not overestimate the impact of feminist evangelicals, as their numbers are relatively small (Hunter, 1987b). This being said, despite their small numbers, Christian feminists may be facilitating significant changes in the way evangelical churches think about and present gender roles.

It is interesting that despite the historic relationship between religion and patriarchal domination, women have tended to be more religious in their beliefs and practices than men.[4] Research suggests that women, despite their rather limited participation in church leadership, are more actively involved in church and its related activities than are men.[5] Women have also used their religious affiliations for their own gain; the suffrage movement was connected to a larger social reform movement that was, in part, rooted in evangelical churches[6] (Gorham, 1976; Kealey, 1979; Banks, 1986; MacHaffie, 1986:98).

The first wave of feminism included two diverse feminisms: maternal feminism[7] and feminism based in equality[8] (Kealey, 1979;

---

[4]Nancy Ammerman found that, despite church doctrine to the contrary, women often assumed the responsibility of spiritual leader in their households (Ammerman, 1987). Steve Warner discovered that it was first women and then their husbands who participated in the Antioch Fellowship (Warner, 1988:121). Notwithstanding their greater involvement (and commitment), women are often granted only secondary status within religious groups; they are excluded from the clergy and assigned domestic service and fund-raising activities (Warner, 1988; Jacobs, 1989; Nason-Clark, 1987).

[5]Bibby, while admitting that differences between the commitment of women and men do exist, cautions us to keep these differences "in proper perspective."

[6]The cost of the suffrage movement to the feminist movement is still debated. Support for suffrage was based on the notion of women as the guardians of society, a role that was largely an extension of their roles as mothers and wives. Maternal or social feminism eventually overtook and subsumed more radical feminist tendencies based in notions of equality (Kealey, 1979).

[7]Maternal feminism, also known as social or domestic feminism, "refers to the conviction that woman's social role as mother gives her the duty and the right to participate in the public sphere" (Kealey, 1979:7).

[8]Natural-rights feminists not only supported an increased public role for women, but also believed that women have the right to define themselves autonomously (Kealey, 1979:7).

Matheson and Lang, 1976). Although both had as their goal the securing of the vote for women, their motives for supporting suffrage were at odds. Maternal feminists (many of whom were evangelical women), in response to what they saw as the moral decay of their society, believed that women, as mothers and nurturers, were specially entrusted (by God) with the task of preserving the moral integrity of society (Kealey, 1979; Gorham, 1976:59; Mitchinson, 1979; MacHaffie, 1986). Without the vote, they could not completely fulfill this duty. Not only were evangelical women active in attempting to secure the vote, they also initiated social welfare programs that were seen as a natural extension of their role as mothers (Pederson, 1995:323; MacHaffie, 1986:98).

Considered in their day to be the more radical faction of the suffragist supporters were those women whose support for the vote and other social and political activism was rooted in a more general commitment to a greater role for women in society. Gradually, the natural-rights feminists' demands for equality were overshadowed by maternal feminists' conviction that women had a special but different calling than men (Roberts, 1979:19; Gorham, 1976:70).[9] Humanism eventually supplanted feminism,[10] and the next four decades were to be quiet ones in the feminist revolution. The first wave of feminism foreshadowed two things in the feminist struggles in years to come. The first was the reemergence of maternal feminism as relational and biologically based feminism using more sophisticated interpretations of psychology and physiology in relation to women. The second was the ever-present tendency in the feminist movement to succumb to humanism.[11]

---

[9]Scott points out that we should not write the history of feminisms as "a story of oscillations between demands for equality and affirmations of difference" (1990:145). Such "snapshots" are too general to accurately portray the processes of feminism. Clearly, the suffragist movement and its theoretical underpinnings cannot be neatly categorized. Gorham also makes this point (1976:52–53). It is also difficult to know what women's motivations for involvement were. Some may simply have seen maternal feminism as the easiest means to an end.

[10]Rhode mentions the postfeminist journal called *Judy*, whose focus was humanism, not feminism (Rhode, 1989:32).

[11]Susan Bordo discusses the dominance of humanism at the end of the first wave of feminism (1990:151–52). For a more recent example, see Menkel-Meadow's (1992) argument for the mainstreaming of feminist legal theory on the basis that feminism is a humanist project. While her argument against the marginalization of feminist legal theory is appealing, we should be wary of the humanist trap to which earlier generations of feminists have succumbed.

The second wave of feminism emerged for a number of reasons, at least in part as a reaction to the male domination of the civil rights and the socialist movements of the 1960s (Rhode, 1989:55). Women grew tired of being relegated to support duties such as cooking and began to assert their desire to be heard. A central concern of the early second-wave feminists, as evidenced by feminist writings of the '60s and '70s,[12] was their desire to control their own bodies, specifically in relation to reproduction.[13]

Women also sought to challenge the "natural" gender division of labor, which had relegated them to the private sphere (Sheilah Martin, 1991:23). As Rhode points out, "The sanctity of domestic life generally called for female exclusion from public pursuits and the law's exclusion from private disputes. Paradoxically, the paternalism that justified confining women to the home did not extend to protecting them within it" (1989:20). The distinction between the public and private spheres is somewhat artificial in that it obscures the diverse nature of women's lives. For example, many women, particularly working-class women and women of color, were present in the public sphere in the workplace. Yet definition of the "proper" private-sphere place of women and the responsibilities ascribed to that place continued to dominate the lives of women, including those whose lived experiences were substantially different from the "ideal." The work women do and the pay women receive for that work continue to reflect the public/private sphere dichotomy, despite feminists' efforts to challenge it.

It is easy to see why second-wave feminism alienated many evangelical women and caused conservative Protestant clergy to take up feminism as a cause to resist. What had previously been celebrated—women's prowess in the domestic sphere—was denigrated, and androgyny was seen as the solution of the day. This focus on sameness was at odds with the evangelical worldview's positing of God-ordained, distinct roles for women. In addition, the abortion debate was also divisive. The ability to destroy that which framed the focal point of many evangelical women's existence, that is, their children, was offensive to many of them and seen as being morally wrong. As a result, evangelical

---

[12]For one example, see *Roles Women Play: Readings Toward Women's Liberation* (Garskof, 1971).

[13]This is not to imply that all women were united in this effort. Issues such as abortion were and continue to be sources of division among feminists.

women did not have the same level of involvement in round two of the feminist struggle as they had had in the first wave.

To discuss feminism as though it were a unified stream of thought is misleading. An almost endless variety of feminisms have emerged during the past century, including liberal feminism (Friedan, 1963), maternal feminism (Ruddick, 1984), relational feminism (Gilligan, 1982), psychoanalytic feminism (Chodorow, 1992), socialist feminism (Jaggar, 1983, 1990; Smith, 1987), radical feminism (MacKinnon, 1989; Daly, 1968, 1973), postmodern feminism (Nicholson, 1990), and so on.[14] While there is often at least some overlap between these feminisms, differences frequently lead to bitter ideological debates and divisions based on which feminism is the real feminism, and consequently, which feminists are the "real" feminists. But these feminisms are not closed categories; they do frequently interrelate, resulting in both frustration and a richer discourse that facilitates analysis that is more sensitive to the lived experiences of women. Each of these feminisms has affected how evangelical women perceive feminism and how they interpret feminism in relation to their own lives. As we have seen in chapter 3, evangelical women valorize their role as mother, and therefore it is not surprising that it is the "difference" feminisms, especially maternal feminism, with which evangelical women can be most closely identified. However, we can identify some common ground between evangelicals and other types of feminism.

Standpoint feminists argue that because of their oppressed position in society, women are uniquely qualified to expose relations of power and control in social life.[15] "The standpoint is not just different from that of the ruling class; it is also epistemologically advantageous" (Jaggar, 1983:370). One of the most valuable contributions of this feminism is its insistence that no position is neutral (Harding, 1987, 1991). Dorothy Smith is well known for her use of standpoint theory in the development of her sociological method of institutional ethnography. For Smith, the institutional control of everyday life is best understood beginning with the standpoint of women (1987). Although their

---

[14]For a very helpful discussion of various strands of feminism, see Valerie Bryson (1992). For an elaboration of the number of "varieties" of feminism, see LeGates (1996).

[15]Dorothy Smith (1987) explains this in terms of what she calls women's bifurcated consciousness, when women's experiences do not fit into existing conceptual practices.

beliefs lack the political implications of standpoint feminism, evangelical women do share the belief that women are uniquely situated in the social world and, as such, they have a unique perspective to offer.

Jane Flax offers a succinct critique of standpoint theory that challenges its underlying assumptions. She identifies those as: (1) that people act rationally in their own interests; (2) that reality has a structure that reason can discover; (3) that the oppressed are not in fundamental ways damaged by their social experience; (4) that women are the "other" (it assumes the otherness that men assign to women); and (5) that women do not participate in relations of domination (1990:56). Standpoint theory holds that women are better able to articulate power inequities simply because they are oppressed.[16]

Carol Gilligan's (1982) research has been the anchor for relational feminists. Relational feminists[17] argue that women in fact develop different ways of assessing and acting in social situations. To women, the preservation of relationships is central to their moral reasoning. Based on Gilligan's work, some feminists have gone on to argue that feminine ethics (ethics of care) are superior to justice as we know it (Jaggar, 1990:249). Historically, evangelical women used the belief in women's different and superior moral skills to argue that women should have the right to vote. Gilligan's research has been criticized for its sample size and for the broadness of its initial conclusions.[18] Her work is valuable, however, if for no other reason than that it prompted feminists to begin exploring possible commonalities in women's ways of interpreting the social world.

"Difference" theories celebrate various aspects of women, whether it be their biologies or reproductive abilities, their mothering, their ethics, or their unique standpoint. Unfortunately, nonfeminist discourses have frequently been able to translate

---

[16]Smart argues that standpoint feminism presents an alternative truth that cannot withstand the concept of multiple realities (1990:200).

[17]Offen uses the term *relational feminism* in a broader way than I do here. She states: "Relational feminism emphasizes the family, the couple, or the mother/child dyad as the basic social unit of the nation...What some call womanliness and others femininity was asserted as an enduring and worthy social characteristic" (1990:18).

[18]As Jaggar points out, Gilligan subsequently revised her conclusions. She "now sees the main significance of her work as consisting in hearing a different voice, a voice that is often, but not exclusively female" (Jaggar, 1990:249). See Fraser and Nicholson (1990:32–33) for a critique of Gilligan.

"different" to mean inferior and in need of protection, both within the context of secular society and within the patriarchal confines of organized religion. While evangelical women often insist that they are different but equal, the rhetoric of conservative Protestantism contains both subtle and overt discriminations based on women's differences.

A focus on difference forces discussion into an endless oppositional debate involving the valuing of men over women. Male is treated as the "norm" or the universal standard against which women are measured.[19] Furthermore, "when equality and difference are paired dichotomously, they structure an impossible choice. If one opts for equality, one is forced to accept the notion that difference is antithetical to it. If one opts for difference, one admits that equality is unattainable" (Scott, 1990:142).[20] As previously mentioned, the "equal but different" approach in many ways resembles the maternal feminism of the early twentieth century, with which evangelical women were closely associated. The presentation of women as different incorporates essentialist tendencies by obscuring the unique experiences of women of color, lesbian women, physically challenged women, and other especially disadvantaged women.[21] In other words, in celebrating difference[22] some theorists assume that all women are, for example, nurturing, or have the potential to be mothers.

The purpose of this brief overview has been to discuss those feminisms that are similar to the manner in which evangelical ideology presents women. Both ideologies present women as different, either biologically, psychologically, in their perspectives,

---

[19]Sheilah L. Martin says: "The choice of the male body as the referent for the equality comparison is neither natural nor logical but derives from a patriarchal social system in which what is 'male' is more highly valued" (1991:128).

[20]We may be beyond a conception of equality as being merely sameness. A more complex understanding of equality may to some extent vitiate Scott's criticism.

[21]Even as I write these categories I realize that they, too, are essentialist: for example, "women of color" is not a homogeneous group. Any analysis will obscure some aspects of some women's lived experience. The key is to be as aware of both what has been left out of an analysis and what has been included.

[22]As Nancy Chodorow's work illustrates, difference is not always to be celebrated. Chodorow does not valorize women as mothers; rather, she points to women's almost exclusive presence in parenting as an explanation for the reproduction of gender as we know it. Maroney criticizes Chodorow for "mother bashing" (1986:57), and Spelman charges her with obscuring race and class (1992). Fraser and Nicholson argue that biological explanations of social phenomena are essentialist and monocausal (1990:28). Yet Chodorow does draw to our attention the possible consequences of woman-only involvement in the so-called private sphere.

or because of their experiences of mothering. Through their involvement in first-wave feminism, which was predicated on women's difference, and their belief that God designed men and women differently, evangelical women remain linked to those strands of feminism that valorize women's differences from men. As we shall see, the "equal but different" approach is reflected in evangelical women's descriptions of feminism.

While there are feminists who espouse an evangelical worldview (Hunter, 1987b), many conservative Christian women are uncomfortable with the feminist label in describing themselves. How do evangelical women understand and define feminism? Do they reject feminism outright, or are there particular tenets of feminism that are more acceptable than others? How is feminist ideology mediated through the responses of evangelical women to the issue of wife abuse? By many feminist standards, a characterization of evangelical Christian women as sympathetic to feminism would be met with, to say the least, skepticism. Conservative Christian women do not pass the "test" on those issues that might be considered to be pillars of feminist activism: abortion, gay and lesbian rights, legal guarantees of equality, and more generally an egalitarian conceptualization of roles and responsibilities for men and women. Many of the participants in my study were actively involved in their local Crisis Pregnancy Centers; almost all were vehemently opposed to the idea that one could be both a practicing gay or lesbian and a Christian; a surprising number did not know what the guarantee of equality was under the Canadian Charter of Rights and Freedoms; and many adhered to a traditional conceptualization of the appropriate roles and responsibilities for women and men. In addition, their language was distinctively not inclusive: God is male,[23] *man* is often used to include women, for example *mankind*, and women are frequently referred to as "ladies." Many of my feminist sisters would have stopped there, rendered judgment of these women as "the Right," and dismissed them as definitely not feminists.[24] But the picture is more complicated when we explore participants' thoughts on feminism and their actions in their everyday lives. What emerges is an interesting picture of women who combine

---

[23]For an in-depth discussion of conceptualizations of God as male and the perceptions of evangelical women, see Pevey (1994).

[24]For an interesting dissection of "the Right," see Klatch (1987).

feminist ideology and Christian commitment to respond to those they encounter who are in need. Like their descriptions of what it means to be an evangelical Christian, conservative Protestant women's understandings of feminism are not monolithic, but reflect the diversity of their everyday experiences.

How do evangelical women think about feminism? What do they see as its central tenets? How do they perceive feminists? Like their maternal feminist foresisters, and similar to difference feminists of today, many of these women honor women's differences. The rhetoric of equality is present, but it is often framed as "equal but different." Women's unique characteristics or differences from men take on an added dimension as falling within God's plan. This sixty-three-year-old full-time worker described feminism in this way:

> To me, if I were to really to participate in that it would be just to get equal status between men and women, not that a woman is a servant or can't go out and get a job or that a woman doesn't belong in a certain profession, perhaps, or something like that, but I also wouldn't be an advocate of the fact that a woman should be out trying to lift the same weight of something as a man, because I think that God created men and women different for different types of…for different roles that they were to have. I mean, emotionally they are made up differently, and so I think that…I'm probably very moderate in that line. (#3)

And:

> It [feminism] means women, and our needs and our wants are just as important as the other sex…on an equal basis, there are some things that women do better than men, I recognize that, and there are things that men do better than women. We have our differences, but I think that we should be treated equally. (#45, age 35)

Another woman stated:

> I think in God's eyes that woman *is* equal to man, but yet there is a union that He devised that the man should be in authority…in line with God's way, in the home where the family, the wife, the children are concerned. And if that's done properly, then you don't feel lesser than or put down by such a husband because they are carrying out their

> duties…to the best they can, understanding God's formula, and that should make a wife and children feel safe, secure …content in knowing that they have someone that will see their best interests. (#2, age 40)

The notion that women are different but equal is cause for celebration in the eyes of evangelical woman.

The acceptability of feminism is not strictly limited to maternal feminism or a celebration of women's difference. Some tenets of feminism are clearly more acceptable to evangelical women than others; while many participants condemned what they called "man-hating" feminism, they were supportive of liberal policies such as (what they described as) equal pay for equal work. Many felt that women should be given the same advancement opportunities as men. Liberal feminism sees the achievement of equality through the extension of legal protections to women, for example, through pay equity legislation.[25] On this issue one participant, after referring to the dictionary definition of feminism, stated:

> …economic—I believe in that. My father and I argue that point. He thinks that a man should be paid more than a woman. And I said why? Well, he's the provider, and if the wife stops working it's…and I said Dad, you know, if two people do the same amount of work do you not think…and he said, well no, I think a woman should be paid less than a man [she laughs]. But no, I believe in equal pay. (#13, age 49)

Support for pay equity is often based in women's own experiences of discrimination in the workplace:

> I worked over at the hospital and it always seemed to me that men got away with doing a lot less work and they got more pay. (#80, age 62)

Some women described how, despite the fact that in many cases they had trained their male coworkers, the male employees were paid significantly more than the female employees.

---

[25]The sameness approach has two fundamental flaws: It fails to address systemic discrimination against women, and it sets up the male standard as the norm.

As Susan Sered points out, it is possible to have equality of the sexes in the relationship of each to God, while at the same time having male dominance over leadership, religious law, and authority in the affairs of the faith community (Sered, 1994:5). Evangelical women believe that in God's eyes males and females are equally valuable to God. However, there is an underlying belief that women think and reason differently. Such a conceptualization of "equal but different" would use difference as justification for the inclusion of women in church leadership, an interesting variation on the traditional view, which excludes women because leadership does not fall within their "unique role."

Evangelical women do not see feminism in rigid yes/no terms: Feminism is seen as a movement with both positive and negative sides. While they agree that feminism has brought about many progressive changes for women, it has also had its costs. This homemaker and mother of four sons said:

> Well, I'm not…100 percent knowledgeable about all of what the feminist beliefs are, although I have myself thought at times that some of what they do believe wouldn't line up with what God teaches us. What I was just talking about a little earlier about put yourself first, look after yourself, ah…you're number one. These seem to be ideas that the feminists sometimes promote within their people. (#2, age 40)

Because feminism is often perceived as promoting self-interest, this brings it into conflict with the JOY (Jesus, others, then you) formula. A Christ-centered life is outwardly focused, not self-interested. As we have already seen, evangelical women emphasize service to others, an attitude that they sometimes see as bringing them into direct opposition to the tenets of feminism. In addition, feminism was sometimes viewed as compromising one's "femininity"; there was also a feeling that feminists had "ruined it" for women by insisting on equal rights. Again, the theme of selfishness emerged, one participant stating that "if we all took a servant attitude, we wouldn't have to worry about rights."

Perhaps the most consistent criticism of feminism is its association with "extremism," including militancy and belligerence. Other associations were "marches and protests," "shaved heads," "briefcases," and "bra burner":

I don't know, again, I just think loud, rude, and obnoxious, and I realize that it's probably not meant to be that way, it's kind of like a woman can do a man's job for equal pay and she deserves it if she can, like if she can do it or whatever…and I believe in that. (#15, age 33)

The idea of women as activists (or at least a particular kind of activist) and extremists is clearly not in keeping with what most evangelical women perceive as being Christian values and principles; however, not all evangelical women associate feminism with extremism. A number of women expressed regret over the association of feminism with extremism, a characterization that they believed was wrong. Some participants were concerned about the narrow focus of feminism, as is illustrated by this comment:

I'm…a little bit troubled by feminism. I think that we should be looking for the dignity of all human beings whether they are male or female…gender. There's men being oppressed in situations as well. It seems to me that feminism represents…women coming together to promote their ideals with the exclusion of men…sort of independent…I'm just troubled by it, I can't really say why. I don't know, I think it narrows your view. Just to have one single issue rather than looking at oppression in general. (#17, age 33)

This attitude is reminiscent of the humanism that eventually overshadowed the first wave of feminism and that rendered the struggle for women's equality nearly dormant for forty years. However, it is also reflective of the current debate in feminism over the essentialist conceptualizations of "woman," which have dominated second-wave feminism. It is interesting that the perception of "narrowness" is often one that is related to conservative Christian women by feminists; each group perceives the other as being single-minded in its pursuits and beliefs. Yet each sees itself as serving others, and, through service, making the world in which they live a better place. The distinction between the two groups is that for evangelical women, service is dedicated to Christ and is a reflection of their Christian commitment. For feminists, service is rooted in a desire to bring about the equality of women, thus ending patriarchy. However, as we shall see later in this chapter, evangelical women themselves do not take an either/or approach to feminism and their faith.

The perceived belittling, rejection, and categorization of men is a concern of evangelical women, even those who call themselves feminists:

> I have said to people that I am a Christian feminist—that I call myself a Christian feminist. But…some of the people who are feminists, in the secular sense, I often think that there is an anti-male sentiment there, you know…for some. Not all of them, not all of the people. I have been associated with some wonderful people who ascribe to the feminist philosophy. I also think people say, oh, "I am not a feminist" without knowing what a feminist is, you know, what feminism is all about. (#91, age 45)

The denigration of men is contrary to beliefs that are central to the worldview of most of these evangelical women: most notably, the idea of Christian love and forgiveness; the God-ordained place of man as the spiritual head of the family; and the sanctity of the heterosexual relationship. In the view of some of the participants, feminists have simply gone too far.

> I think God intended women to have a particular role in society and to be respected, but I also think that perhaps in some feminist movements they are going too far with that, so its like a vendetta. (#3, age 63)

This 32-year-old homemaker, who described herself as a latent feminist, stated, about active feminism:

> There becomes a really ugly side to it, a sort of hatred of men for what they stand for and what they've done, for what they've done to women, which is all very true, but it seems to be an ugly sort of character in striving for women's equality. (#14)

Traditionalists are likely to see feminism as challenging God-ordained roles for women. The Bible, in their view, prescribed women as thinkers and peacemakers and men as the "stronger sex." The following woman's comment is representative of those participants' views: "In the Bible, man is the head of the household. Most feminists would not be willing to accept the man as the head of the household" (#19, age 38). In a similar vein, some women were willing to accept some tenets of feminism, but were unwilling to consider anything as "radical" as a woman pastor. Others were supportive of inclusive language, as long as God remains male. But some participants mentioned that they thought that changing the language of the Bible goes too far, and that feminists sometimes had too much of their own agenda and not enough of God's.

Evangelical women were not, however, overwhelmingly negative in their discussions of feminism; like other groups of women, they accept some tenets, like pay equity, while rejecting those aspects that they perceive as the more extreme elements of feminism. The description of feminism by this forty-seven-year-old who works part time as a data processor aptly illustrates the complex way in which feminism has impacted on her life as a Christian:

> I mean, if feminism was women demanding the rights that they should have to begin with, without having to demand them, you know, if that's what feminism is...women saying, look, I deserve more than I'm getting in this world, you know, I'm a person, my feelings and my rights are equal to my husband's, you know, if I'm doing the same job as he's doing in the workforce, then I should be paid the same money. If he thinks that he can go off and golf six days a week but I can't go out to dinner one day a week, if that's feminism, then that's fine, I'm all for that. I demand my own rights, I'm, as far as I am concerned, totally equal in my home, and I demand equal time [she laughs] and that is definitely reconcilable to the Bible, as far as I'm concerned. We should not have that side that's gone to the point where their main thing seems to be belittling the role of men and putting themselves above that. And sometimes I think that's what people will perceive as feminism. (#1)

The positive aspects of feminism include the belief that it has opened choices for women, that there is nothing wrong with having a career, that women's viewpoints are important and should be heard, and that it is good to believe in yourself. A few women noted that part of Christ's ministry was to liberate women, and that Jesus taught that women are important. A number of women noted that there are strong women in scripture, and that God respects men and women equally. One woman stated that "being a feminist doesn't make me less in God's eyes."

A feminist to me is standing up for being a woman, and realizing that…that was part of Christ's ministry—is liberating women from the bondage they were under. (#42, age 46)

Well, I think you can be both a feminist and a Christian. I think that…God has as much respect for women as he does for men, and loves us both equally, and that he didn't intend for one to be in this power struggle over the other, and a lot of feminist issues I applaud and I'm grateful that the feminist movement has done a lot, I think, for women, and brought us up out of the dark ages. (#48, age 32)

Those who affirm the compatibility of feminism and Christianity draw on comparisons between Christian principles like respect for others and feminist goals like respect for women. Some women reflected on their own position; either they called themselves Christian feminists or they felt that they held at least some feminist viewpoints. As one woman put it, as long as Christ comes first, burning one's bra and paying for one's meals does not preclude one's being a Christian.

God-related comments were used to both justify involvement in the feminist movement and to criticize feminist affiliation. The perception that feminism was or might be explicitly contradictory to scripture or to Christian teachings was seen both in respect to the appropriate roles for men and women and in women's relationship to God:

I don't think you could be a totally committed Christian, 'cause to me commitment means following all…you know, being exactly what God wants you to be, and I don't feel that that's part of God's plan, I may be wrong, but I don't see it in my scripture.

[Interviewer: What does scripture say women should be?]

Well, as I said before, as a helpmate to our spouse, that spouse being a man…Now that's in the family relationship; in the world I have no problem with women doing tasks that are also, you know, that men can do and that only men used to do, but ah, as far as women being bosses over men, I don't have a problem with that in the world, but in the church I don't believe...or in the home even, I don't think it should be the situation. (#82, age 41)

For traditionalists, involvement in feminism raises concerns over the possibility of tarnishing one's witness: "I think there's a limit. I think that...a woman can go overboard to the point where it is going to affect her Christian witness. So I think she has to be extremely careful—she has to know where to draw the line" (#27, age 46). Conflicts with scripture were also articulated in relation to the self-centeredness that was often associated with feminism by the women who participated in this study. Arguing for one's own value, stated one woman, goes against Christian character and scripture.

Because of the primacy of obedience to God in the evangelical worldview, anything that competes with or challenges christo-centrism or comes into conflict with God's word is viewed as contrary to Christian commitment. Other specific contradictions mentioned included the exploitation of men, abortion, and staying at home; some women felt that feminism had made it difficult for women to stay at home. A few participants felt that feminism compromises one's femininity; one woman stated that "it's nicer to be *feminine* than *feminist*."

The impact of the media on evangelical women's perceptions of feminism is profound. It is quite clear that much of what women perceive as constituting feminism has been gleaned from what they hear and see from the media.

Um, I probably wouldn't consider myself a feminist because of what the media says a feminist is, and I don't want to be associated with...that, you know, type of definition, which to me is very selfish and one-sided. (#25, age 35)

Such media-generated perceptions often alienate evangelical women:

A lot of people would describe me as a feminist. I don't really feel I'm a true feminist, because I like to stay at home, and I like to take care of my children, and I get a lot of enjoyment out of that. But I also like to be in the work force too. I don't want to be here and just thought of as a mother, although I think it's a very important job, and I want to do it the best I can, but I want to have other interests outside of that role. (#48)

Extremism becomes a central theme in sorting out which aspects of feminism are reconcilable with an evangelical world-view. It is clear that the media plays a role in this:

I guess the extreme fundamentalism of the feminists... again, it's just through what you pick up in the newspaper or the TV or whatever, I think they've taken it too far by changing God into a woman or not letting a man hold the door open for you, or things like that, I think they're just plain stupid...but I do think though that as a woman that you are equal to a man and I think that everybody's got their special gifts for one thing or another...I do believe, of course, that women should vote, and that women can hold office, and women can be deacons and ministers ...but to be on the bandwagon all the time about women's issues when there's...when there's other things that are important.

[Interviewer: So you see feminism as incorporating a variety of things?]

Yeah, like there's no clear-cut definition, there's extremes, it's almost the same thing as somebody saying that they're Christian, you kind of have to find out what church they go to to find out where they're actually fittin' in. (#76, age 34)

It is ironic that the same language—such as "extremism" and "fundamentalism"—that feminists sometimes use to describe evangelicals is reflected in this woman's description of feminism. One woman got up during the interview and looked up the definition of feminism in her dictionary. It stated "advocacy of political, economic and social equality for women...a feminist is an advocate of feminism...," a definition that surprised her.

From the perspective of evangelical women, feminism is a complex ideology featuring both negative and positive aspects. It is viewed as sometimes going too far, especially when it denigrates men or is "extremist":

My definition is not anger-driven towards men. I'm not a man-hater, I'm not a husband-basher. I feel like women are a vital part of society, and they're a vital part of the family, and they are to be respected, and loved and enjoyed. (#18)

No, I like having the door held for me, and those kinds of little niceties that go with...I don't know, weak female, I hope is not what I mean, because I don't think I'm that. (#46, age 27)

However, despite their reservations, most evangelical women readily acknowledge the positive contribution feminism has made to women's lives, including their own.

Though feminism was associated with equality, it was often tempered in definition to mean "equal but different." Feminism is most positively viewed when it allows women to maintain their distinctiveness, or difference, from men. Overt and public political acts, such as marches and protests, are the feature of feminism that makes most evangelical women uncomfortable. This is in keeping with their emphasis on peace; indeed, throughout the interviews some participants described women as "peacemakers." Actions that alienate, rather than reconcile, are seen as being outside the Christian worldview. For the most part, evangelical women support the goals of feminism, such as equal pay and an end to the denigration of women in society, but they reject much of the rhetoric associated with the feminist movement.

As a feminist, I was sometimes taken aback by the narrow description of feminism I heard from evangelical women. Their perception seemed to focus on man-hating, loud-mouthed protesters who burned their bras, given the smallest amount of encouragement. From Hunter's research (1987b) I knew that there is a small but vocal feminist presence among evangelical women. I was intrigued by this, especially since much of the action I had observed among evangelical women in relation to the issue of wife abuse was similar to that which takes place in the secular feminist community. In considering their own commitment to feminism, evangelical women are cautious. Ultimately, their commitment to Christ is paramount, and therefore anything that is seen to conflict with it is reworked or rejected. Sometimes the goals of feminism are accepted, but the use of the label "feminist" for themselves is going too far. In this way, evangelical women selectively appropriate those aspects of feminism that meet their needs. Like their interpretation of the doctrine of submission, feminism is interpreted in ways that make sense to women as they go through daily life.

A surprisingly large number of the participants in this study identified themselves in some measure with feminist ideologies, although they often perceive themselves as being outside the mainstream feminist movement. Though they were sometimes cautious in their commitment, there was not the degree of hostility toward feminism that one might expect. What these women seemed to have more trouble with was the feminist movement, which they tended to characterize rather narrowly. However, while evangelical women may support feminist goals, and even use the label "feminist" to describe themselves, it is their Christian worldview, not feminist ideology, that prescribes and explains their daily activities. As one woman put it, it's okay to be a feminist, as long as being a Christian comes first.

What emerges from women's discussions of their personal involvement with feminism is a picture of varying acceptance of feminist goals and activities, with an emphasis on moderation. There is general support for the equality of women, although equality often incorporates the notion that women are different from men. In addition, there is specific support for pay equity and equality of treatment for women in the paid labor force. An underlying theme here was the notion of wholeness, or the idea that women are humans beings and as such should be able to be all that they can be.

While some women did not see feminism as posing a threat to the idea that women are different, others saw this as the primary barrier to their involvement in the feminist movement. Feminism was seen as stripping women of their unique roles; homemaking and feminism were often viewed as being incompatible. Militancy, extremism, and man-hating were also seen as creating an atmosphere within feminism that is at odds with the evangelical worldview.

Although Hunter (1987b) points to the presence of feminism among evangelical women, he also qualifies his discussion by suggesting that by no means is it a dominant, or even prominent, ideology within conservative Protestantism. Christian feminists, though passionate about their Christian commitment, also recognize that women have been treated as less than equal within the church. As Stacey and Gerard put it, "Evangelical feminists are serious about both their evangelicalism and their feminism, and each belief system modifies the other" (1990:101). Christian feminists do not see feminism and Christianity as incompatible; rather, feminism offers women hope in their journey to spiritual wholeness and as fully participating members of the church community. Faith Martin writes: "Somehow it isn't nice for Christian women to ask for their rights. We've been told that a lot. But more and more women are finding themselves uncomfortable with their role. Is this what God intended for my life—or is this for men's convenience?" (1988:5). Christian feminists use the Bible and Christ's example to argue for women's equality; Dorothy Pape says, "Nowhere is there any statement of the inferiority of woman, nor are there any lists of do's and don'ts applying to her in particular" (1976:19). Some Christian feminists, like Letha Scanzoni and Nancy Hardesty, argue that women should not be bound by "difference," but rather that every woman should have the chance "to develop and test her inner capabilities without having someone say, 'That isn't ladylike'" (1974:85).

Though the majority of evangelical women do not see feminism and Christianity as incompatible, they are not comfortable with all aspects of feminism. In particular, associations with "radical" or "stark" feminism are viewed negatively, and extremism and militancy are viewed as incompatible elements. There is an ambiguity in evangelical women's thinking about feminism; they approach feminism selectively, picking and choosing those tenets that are seen as being compatible with an evangelical worldview.

Discussions about feminism highlight the differences between the traditionalists, feminists, and moderates. While evangelical feminists use the examples of Christ and the Bible to support the compatibility of evangelicalism and feminism, traditionalists draw on scripture to point out women's proper roles and the ways in which feminism is contrary to God's intended plan for women. Traditionalists highlight the inherent contradictions between the two worldviews using a blanket description of radical feminism as representative of all feminism. Rejection of liberal feminism is consistent for traditionalists in that they believe that women, whose primary role is that of mother, should have extremely limited roles in the workforce. Moderates are careful not to reject feminism but are cautious in their acceptance of what they perceive as "extremist" aspects of the feminist movement.

Although both ideologies have a tradition of viewing women as different from men, a number of tensions between feminism and the evangelical worldview emerged in the discussions about feminism. The first related to the perception that feminists are self-centered and selfish, which is in opposition to the JOY formula adhered to by conservative Protestant Christians. Another tension is the perception that feminists are somehow anti-child and that they diminish the role of mother, in contrast to the emphasis on the primacy of the mothering role within the evangelical worldview. The perceived denigration of men is also a focus of criticism of feminism. Finally, extremism and divisiveness, which are antithetical to evangelical women's commitment to peace-making and reconciliation, are associated with the feminist movement.

This exploration of feminism and evangelical women should not be read to imply that evangelical women should or should not describe themselves as feminists. Rather, given evangelical women's historical roots in feminist activism, it is important to examine the links between their past and present approaches to social problems. The belief that women have a unique role to fulfill enabled evangelical women to justify their entry into the political arena to fight for the right to vote (among other things) in the early-twentieth-century first wave of feminism. Their present-day links to feminist activism are less clear. Though evangelical women support many of the goals of feminism, they are uneasy with the public image of feminism and with some feminist methods, which they characterize as "extreme" or "militant." These data reveal that the relationship between feminism and conservative Protestant ideology is complex, and the characterization of evangelical women as antifeminist is inaccurate.

7

Evangelical Women as Activists: Their Response to Violence Against Women[1]

As described in chapter 3, evangelical women are reluctant to call the activities they engage in pursuant to their commitment to service "activism." The issue of violence against women provides us with an interesting case study of the ways in which evangelical women approach a serious social problem. While not mobilized to stop violence in the same way as the transition house movement, evangelical women do contribute to the fight against violence by consistently offering support to victims.

In order to talk about the response of evangelical women to the problem of violence against women, it is essential to first have an understanding of the ways in which conservative Protestant churches in general have responded to this pervasive social problem. While organized religion has been slow to respond to the problem of violence against women, there is a growing literature by clergy, Christian counselors, and Christian researchers (Morris, 1988; Strom, 1986; McDill, 1991; Fortune, 1991) that addresses violence in Christian families. In addition, a number of training programs have been developed to help clergy deal with

---

[1] This chapter was co-authored with Dr. Nancy Nason-Clark.

abuse as they minister to their congregations on a daily basis. While these writings are unequivocal in their condemnation of violence within Christian families as being contrary to God's plan, they also often emphasize themes such as reconciliation. Unfortunately, such resources may offer little assistance to clergy who have limited or no understanding of abusive relationships, and there is a paucity of data that measures the incidence of abuse among Christian families. Studies that measure the amount of violence against women in society are generally fraught with problems, and religious communities are equally as difficult to conduct such research within. In the following sections we will examine in greater detail the response of evangelical women to abuse, as well as explore the response of clergy to the issue of violence against women.

Defining Abuse

One important mediating factor between patriarchal ideologies like submission and understandings of violence against women is experience. More than 90 percent of the evangelical women I have talked to have known a woman who has been abused. Participants have had contact with women who have been physically, emotionally, mentally, and financially abused. Evangelical women do not derive their complex definitions of abuse from abstract sources; rather, their understanding is rooted in their contact with women who have suffered abuse in the family context. This woman describes her role in relation to an abused woman as a listener. When asked about the nature of the abuse, she responded:

> One was, yes, he classified himself as very, a very astute Christian, this wasn't the, ah, verbal abuse in that, but it was certainly being submissive, calling you master of the house. "You are the servant, I give you so much money, that's all you can have." (#88, age 50)

Another participant, who had "baked up a storm" of muffins for the day her friend had intended to leave her abusive husband, describes the nature of her friend's abusive relationship:

> And he just, you know, it went further and further and further. And so towards the later years in their marriage it

was more, it was the kind of abuse that I think it must be the hardest for, um, he would never speak to her. And I mean they'd go weeks without him uttering a word to her. Um, and if the words were uttered, they were, not a nice thing, you know, like "You're a slob, you're a blah, blah, blah," you know that type of stuff. And, ah, and she isn't, I mean by any stretch of the imagination. And so I think she had a really hard job, I think that kind of abuse is really hard in the way that, when you put it into words, it doesn't sound that big, do you know what I mean? And so I think when she would put it into words or try to describe to somebody what it was, a lot of people might not understand that that might not be abuse, you know. (#30, age 36)

It is clear that evangelical women have extensive contact with abused women, not only simply by knowing them, but through their provision of support to them. Moreover, in their descriptions of the abuse suffered by the women with whom they have had contact, they incorporate understandings and definitions of abuse that transcend physical abuse alone.

For evangelical women, abuse is most obviously physical abuse, but it also incorporates more insidious aspects such as power and control. Included in their descriptions of abuse are psychological abuse such as belittling, putting down, neglect, and treating a wife as a servant and not a partner. This pastor's wife described a number of aspects of wife abuse:

Hum…wife abuse…betrayal, abandonment, um… physical beating, that's what comes to mind. Certainly I feel that shouting and name calling…and I'm talking serious, serious stuff…demeaning a person's self-image, with the intent to beat the person down, quote unquote, to lower their self-esteem. (#9, age 60)

Such descriptions indicate both a wide definition of abuse and also a sophisticated understanding of the implications of abusive behavior. Physical abuse is a taken-for-granted aspect of this definition. Women who have been abused often report that the more difficult aspect of abuse from which to recover is emotional abuse.

A number of women specifically mentioned aspects of power and control, like being denied the right to seek employment, financial abuse, being made a prisoner in one's home, and domineering behavior. This thirty-year-old stay-at-home mother of two defined abuse in this way:

> Um, it takes on two facets for me, physical and emotional. So physical, obviously, someone hurting, as my five-year-old would say, hands are for helping, not for hurting. These would be hurting hands. And emotional, I just talked to a friend who has a friend whose husband does not give her an allowance unless his...the house is clean...He takes her grocery shopping, he's the one who writes the checks, she gets no money, it's almost like she's held hostage, okay? He's calling the shots on things, but you can't put your finger on anything to say hey, he's abusive...you know what I mean? But she is just kept right under that toe. So that's to me a form of emotional, you know, put downs, you're not keeping the place clean enough, and you know, there's so many things. Anything I think that keeps a person from their freedom, you know? Not choosing what they want. (#23)

Related to emotional abuse are considerations of a woman's wholeness and well-being. One woman, who had suspected that a coworker was being emotionally abused, described her understanding of wife abuse:

> I think any sort of behavior toward a woman that makes her feel less of herself. Like she is no good. Anything that would humiliate her, anything that would strip her of her pride, make her feel less than she knows that she is. It's not very long before people begin to believe that they are less than what they know that they are. (#1, age 47)

Definitions of abuse that focus on wholeness include not treating a person as a whole or equal person, anything that demeans or degrades, failure to encourage and edify, and devastation to the heart. The range and comprehensiveness of definitions of abuse offered by evangelical women are impressive. Most have no formal training on the issue but have seen the impact of abuse on friends, family, and coworkers. This experiential basis of comprehension lends a credibility to their definitions.

While understanding of the nature of abusive relationships varied, this woman expressed a sensitivity to the difficulties faced by women who live in abusive relationships:

> [T]he other thing I think people really have to realize is that if my husband assaulted me tomorrow, for the first time in my life, and with all the things I know about—that's not how abuse happens, but let's just say for an argument, ah, that that's what happened, and then I had to sort of come to terms with maybe having to end the relationship because the relationship changed. You know, I know in my own mind I would have a lot of difficulty with that. I really would, and so, when you hear people say, you know, why doesn't she just leave the relationship, I mean, you invest so much. Women invest so much in their relationships, its not just a simple matter of saying that's the end of it. (#91, age 45)

This sort of discussion acknowledges the agency exercised by women who live in abusive relationships without minimizing the harm suffered by women. It also reflects on the broader social patterns that are reality for many women. Relationships are important to women to the extent that they are unwilling to walk away from their partners, even when the partners are abusive.[2]

There are a number of interesting points that emerge from the responses of the participants: first, their definitions of abuse are sophisticated and sensitive, perhaps more so than one might have expected within the context of a conservative Christian worldview. Most women have not attended training sessions or worked in transition houses or other situations in which knowledge about abuse would be required or acquired. Their definitions emerge from their life experiences as friends, sisters, daughters, neighbors, and coworkers. Their discussions of abuse are reflective, thoughtful, and sensitive. There is a connectedness between "real life" and their definitions, which we see emerging again in their hands-on response to victims of abuse.

Second, evangelical women are attuned to the various forms that abuse can take, demonstrated by their frequent identification

---

[2]One aspect of this is also that women are socialized to see their own worth in relation to men—without a relationship, no matter how bad, many women feel worthless. This may be exacerbated in a faith community that emphasizes a very narrow definition of family.

of the emotional and unseen types and consequences of abuse. This is important because the impact of these types of abuse is especially devastating. Emotional abuse leaves women with little self-esteem and a reduced ability to negotiate day-to-day life. Acknowledgment of the debilitating consequences of emotional abuse is central to the provision of support to abused women.

Finally, unlike clergy, evangelical *women* are not at all uncomfortable with language that specifically names women as the recipients of violence by men or that names men as the perpetrators. While some women did raise the possibility of violence against men, they were not unwilling to discuss wife abuse or violence against women, and they did not rename it as family violence. Naming the problem is an important facilitator in relations with secular service providers such as transition houses. Church women have eliminated this barrier to working cooperatively with secular service providers.

Explaining Abuse

Given their sophisticated definitions of abuse, how do evangelical women explain abuse? Does their Christian worldview impact on the way they make sense of violence against women? Feminist explanations for abuse focus on power and control. While evangelical women do appropriate these explanations, they are tempered by a Christian worldview that places human failings in the context of sin, resulting in a dichotomy between explanations that are sacred and those that are secular.

Sacred reasons include sin, the failure to turn to Christianity, the fact that we live in a fallen world, and misunderstandings of scripture as causes of abuse. Sacred explanations link the cause of abuse to spiritual deficiencies, either at an individual level or as a world "problem." Secular explanations rely on social scientific research, which can range from individual pathology to structural reasons such as patriarchy. Sin as an explanation is illustrated by this woman's comment:

> Well, sin, it goes back to sin. As long as there is sin, there will be wars, there will be people murdering, and there will be wife abuse. (#50, age 47)

And:

> I think it just exists because people are so...sinful, I mean that sounds so scriptural and so on, but I think it's true, I

mean, there is sin in the world and that is one way that it comes out…People are basically, and getting more so, very, very selfish, and, and I think so many things that happen in this world come about because you're selfish. Wife abuse comes about in my mind because a husband does not want to put himself out for his wife. He wants to be number one, he's very self-centered, he doesn't want to have to think of someone else who is…as important as him. He wants to be the boss, and this is the way that he shows it. (#49, age 39)

Other sacred explanations include the fact that scripture is sometimes misinterpreted to endorse abuse, as well as the possibility that some women misunderstand the meaning of submission. Abuse is linked to marriages that are not based on scripture. Participants also noted that we live in a fallen world that is full of evil and the influence of Satan.

Evangelical women are most likely to call on sacred explanations when reflecting on violence in Christian families. In contrast to the 19 percent of spiritually related explanations to account for the existence of abuse in the world generally, two thirds of the responses that sought to explain abuse in Christian families relied on sacred factors. In Christian families, sacred explanations such as the humanness of Christians, the relationship of violence to God's plan for family life, and a failure to turn to God outweigh the explanatory value of secular factors like the intergenerational cycle of violence. Abuse within Christian families is seen as being contrary to God's plan for family living:

> I don't think it's in God's plan for family living at all, to have, to have an abusive relationship, at all. I think that if anybody uses that that they're just distorting the scriptures, that the man, whether they believe the man should be in charge or not…I just can't understand how people can use scriptures to justify it or say that…it's in God's plan, the woman should stay because she's being abused because… you know, to keep the family together and that…I don't think that's in God's plan at all. (#48, age 32)

Like their pastors, evangelical women dichotomize their understandings of violence in Christian families and in society generally (Nason-Clark, 1995a). One implication of this is that solutions to abuse may be bifurcated as well: sacred solutions for

Christian families, secular solutions for those who are not Christian (Nason-Clark, 1995a).

Surprisingly, evangelical women often turn to secular, specifically feminist, explanations for abuse, which include power and control by men and patriarchy. In part, this may be explained by the failure of the evangelical worldview to make adequate sense of the existence of abuse.

> Well, I think it exists because our society has generally been male dominated and they've always been in positions of power and control and, now that this society is really shifting…I think abuse has been around forever, but now that society is shifting and women are very educated as men are, that we realize that this is not something that we have to take. (#48, age 32)

Evangelical women recognize that traditional roles for women sometimes leave them with less power than men, and they are thus more vulnerable to abuse. Patriarchal social structures, in which women are viewed as inferior and thought of as men's property, are also seen as explanations for the existence of abuse. The economically disadvantaged position of women is viewed as a contributing factor to women's powerlessness. A number of women integrated both feminist and sacred explanations in their responses:

> But we have, in our patriarchal [society], we have said, men are the leaders, men are the head, men have authority, women are supposed to submit, ummm, that doesn't happen to be what scripture says, but that's how we've interpreted it. So…I think that's a lot of it, some people blame Christianity for it, but that isn't what Christ taught, it's how we've interpreted it, the men who were the leaders in the church interpreted it [she laughs] how, I don't think you can lay it at Christ's door. (#70, age 51)

Despite their Christian worldview, evangelical women, like their clergy, rely predominantly on secular explanations to understand the occurrence of abuse in the world around them. While sacred explanations are not an insignificant explanatory factor, they are not as important as feminist explanations such as power and control in understanding the existence of wife abuse in the world. As we have already seen, evangelical women are willing to appropriate those portions of feminist discourse that they can reconcile with their Christian worldview. In this case, power and control over another person prevent that person from reaching her full potential and may interfere in her relationship with God. This modest reliance on their sacred worldview is again reflected in their responses to how wife abuse can be eliminated.

Evangelical women's definitions of abuse are comprehensive and inclusive, though perhaps surprisingly secular. Their explanations for abuse in society generally, while including sacred components, rely most heavily on interpretations that are typically associated with feminism, namely power, control, and patriarchy. To a great extent the complexity of understanding about the problem of wife abuse among this group of evangelical women is rooted in their extensive contact with victims of abuse, and in their own experiences as abused women.

Similar to findings on clergy and violence (see Nason-Clark, 1997), we see that there is a bifurcation among conservative Christians in relation to explaining violence: Sacred explanations predominate in their reflections on the reasons for the existence of abuse in Christian families, while sociological factors loom large in their explanations of violence in the secular world. Unlike clergy, both in their language and in their identification of solutions for abuse, women were willing to emphasize the role of men as perpetrators of violence against women. In summary, evangelical women weave both sacred and secular explanations, under-standings, and solutions through their approach to the problem of woman abuse.

Responding to Abuse

Clergy are often criticized for responding to abused women by telling them to "go home and pray about it." The frequency with which clergy actually give such advice remains a matter for empirical investigation, but it remains a common perception nonetheless. In contrast, the response of evangelical women can be best characterized as practical rather than spiritual. Very few evangelical women suggest prayer or other sacred solutions (greater church involvement, for example) as the solution to violence against women. Social changes, such as harsher penalties for abusers, better support for abused women (including more shelters), and working together to find alternatives to prison, are named as viable solutions to the problem of woman abuse. More than one quarter of these women felt that violence will never be eliminated, perhaps reflecting their belief that we live in a sin-filled world, but also revealing the extent to which evangelical women appreciate the seriousness of this pervasive social problem.

The women I talked to respond to abused women on the basis of a general understanding about the nature of abusive relationships, as well as an appreciation for the needs of individual women. While they are often reluctant to give advice, evangelical women do offer information about available services. In the rare situations when they feel qualified, evangelical women will offer counseling. The following woman's discussion of advice reflects the approach transition house workers use with women who come to shelters:

> I really don't agree with people offering advice. I do agree with people offering information and suggestions. Because I think that when you offer advice you are disabling a person to make their own decision, but if you offer them information, they're able to weigh and say, okay, I have this information, I have this information, I can make an informed decision. So I guess I would give her information. (#23, age 30)

This woman had also provided practical support, such as food, transportation, and baby-sitting. This is not to say that there is never any advice offered. Some women report being directive with victims of abuse.

> Well, I don't know, I guess at one point when she left him…like it was just a temporary thing, and…maybe he actually put her out that time, maybe, and I guess I advised her that maybe she could try it on her own, I didn't recommend, like, transition house or anything like that because her mother knew of the situation and she was very willing to put them up. (#31, age 39)

Advice is sometimes tempered according to the nature of the abuse suffered.

> If their life is in danger, if I feel that they are really, ah, probably in danger, I would advise them to get out of the relationship, but if it's not a situation like that, sometimes you advise them to seek counseling. (#90, age 67)

Support often take very practical forms, as is evidenced by this woman's experience:

> And so I offered her to come and stay with me until she found a different place to stay and whatnot, and she needed to go to court—she took him to court, and she wanted me to go as a witness, and I had never done anything like that before and I was petrified, anyway I told her that I would go, to help her, and so I did. She, ah, she stayed with me, oh, for quite a while—two or three months. She finally got herself straightened away, away from him. (#39, age 40)

Secular interventions also include going with women to their physicians, lawyers, social service agencies, or court.

Despite their commitment to marriage, evangelical women are willing to intervene in abusive situations to facilitate the separation of the abused woman from her husband. Some women take risks to accomplish this:

> I certainly have had her and her children in the house until we sneaked back over to the home and got the liquor out of the house and I got the firing pin out of a gun…yeah, I guess I have…literally been involved…and got a call at the same time saying he was back, on the way, coming up the road, and oh, yeah, I have been involved, yeah. (#73, age 52)

While this type of intervention may not be the most prudent course of action, it is clear that taking risks to help a victim of abuse is not out of the question. In the course of helping women to leave their abusers, evangelical women provide transportation and shelter, help in moving, and help in finding a job.

Material support also includes food, clothing, money, loaning of personal items, and offering childcare on both short- and long-term bases. The range of support does sometimes include counseling, but only when the woman feels she has the qualifications. Support is holistic, including both emotional and material resources.

One of the more intriguing aspects of support is described by women as "offering a listening ear." There is a recognition that sometimes abused women simply need to talk.

> My advice is to seek professional counseling, see that the children are taken care of, I think the most I emphasize is professional counseling. I don't perceive myself as being trained, but sometimes people, they just don't want to have professional counseling, they accept that they are going to live with it, they just need someone to listen to them. (#37, age 34)

Emotional support takes a number of forms, including trying to build self-esteem in the abused woman. This thirty-five-year-old nurse described her support to a friend, for whom she had also offered prayer support:

> Basically supportive in that…she was doing the right thing by pressing charges, and that she shouldn't feel guilty because he was going to be losing his, ah…if found guilty, which he was, he lost his career, he was no longer, he's no longer a policeman, because he was found guilty of these charges. And that, you know, that wasn't her…I just offered that, you know, you shouldn't be feeling guilty about this because you did not do this. And it wasn't because of her pressing charges that he lost the job, it was because of what he did is why he lost the job. (#48)

This thirty-two-year-old woman describes a similar intervention:

> Ah, it was a matter of just really kind of listening to her and just letting her talk and helping her to see that these things she's struggling with are not her fault, because there's a real tendency to think that the woman is at fault somehow, that, you know, she's a terrible person and she's done something wrong or she must have asked for it. So really to just to let her talk her way through it and to talk about the different situations and different experiences and to, um, to listen mostly and to correct her when she started things like "You know, I know I deserve this," or "Um, I know I'm not a really good person." And when she started falling into that pattern of, of demeaning herself, because that's what he had done to her for so many years, that she had just started believing that. Um, and so you know,

correcting her whenever she started falling into that trap of, of saying those things again and, "No you're not a bad person, you know, and what he did to you is not acceptable." And just really reminding her and reminding her again and again until she started to believe it for herself. (#63)

For evangelical women, holistic support necessarily includes a spiritual aspect. However, only one woman I interviewed used her involvement in such a situation as an opportunity to witness directly. This is the case even though many of the women to whom support is offered are not themselves evangelical Christians. Prayer is an integral component of the "support package," but it is offered together with other forms of support. While evangelical women do pray with those to whom they offer support, this is usually only done when the abused woman shares a Christian worldview.

[W]ith a Christian woman you could encourage them to, you know, pray about it, and that sort of thing, whereas a non-Christian would not want to listen to that necessarily, you know, so that would be the difference there, you know, but as far as the help that you would give them, I mean or whatever, that wouldn't change. (#85, age 50)

In their support of women who live in abusive relationships, evangelical women combine sacred and practical strategies. How can we make sense of their action? Is it grounded in a feminist commitment to end women's oppression? More likely, it is a reflection of evangelical women's commitment to service, which includes not only public service, but also involves identifying and meeting the needs of those they encounter in their everyday lives. Though evangelical women often understand the causes of violence against women in light of feminist explanations such as power and control, few of them politicize their action.[3]

The Response of Clergy

The research described in this book was connected to a larger research initiative undertaken by the Religion and Violence

---

[3]One woman was involved with her local transition house; another reported writing a letter to the federal minister of justice in protest of allowing drunkenness as a defense of sexual assault.

124 Shared Beliefs, Different Lives

Research Team of the Muriel McQueen Fergusson Center for Family Violence Research at the University of New Brunswick.[4] The Religion and Violence Research Team's program of research has sought to examine the role of faith communities and their leaders in responding to the pain and suffering caused by wife abuse and other forms of family violence. While the team's research has included a variety of denominations, the results described here will focus exclusively on data obtained from evangelical clergy and laypeople. We have employed a variety of research methodologies to examine wife abuse and contemporary evangelical churches, including mailed questionnaires, in-depth interviews, telephone surveys, focus groups, and community consultations. Our desire was to explore how clergy, church women, abuse victims, transition house workers, and ordinary men and women of evangelical church congregations understood and responded to the needs presented by victims of violence.[5]

We received mailed surveys from more than 340 evangelical clergy (a 70 percent response rate), conducted in-depth interviews with 100 of these pastors, and organized 30 focus groups of between 5 and 20 church women, for a total of 247 church women. Taken together, these data sources paint a rather comprehensive picture of how evangelical congregations are responding to violence in their own midst and within the communities where their churches are located.

So what results have we obtained? How are evangelical churches and their leaders responding to the myriad of issues raised by wife abuse and other forms of family violence? Do evangelical pastors send women back to home environments

[4]The Religion and Violence Research Team was established in 1992 by Nancy Nason-Clark, who has served as coordinator since its inception. Team members include: Terry Atkinson, Lori Beaman, Lois Mitchell, Christy Hoyt, and Sheila McCrea, plus several graduate student assistants. Financial support for the research of the team has been provided by the Louisville Institute for the Study of Protestantism and American Culture, the Social Sciences and Humanities Research Council of Canada, the Department of the Solicitor General, Secretary of State Canada, Status of Women Canada, the Lawson Foundation, the Constant Jacquet Award of the Religious Research Association, the Fichter Award of the Association for the Sociology of Religion, the Muriel McQueen Fergusson Center for Family Violence Research, and the University of New Brunswick Research Fund. Financial and in-kind contributions have been provided by the participating denominations.

[5]The series of studies have included the United Baptist Convention of the Atlantic Provinces, the Atlantic District of the Wesleyan Church, the Maritime Conference of the United Church, the Maritime Division of the Salvation Army, and the Anglican Church of Canada in New Brunswick.

where their safety and self-esteem cannot be assured? Do church women pray for victims but fail to offer them a spare room for the night or emotional support at their point of need? Should we be optimistic or pessimistic about the advice that the average evangelical pastor or church woman offers to a battered wife and her children?

Through our survey and interview data with evangelical clergy, we have learned that there are both blindspots and signs of sensitivity in terms of the reaction of the average pastor to a woman victim of abuse (Nason-Clark, 1996). Ministerial sensitivity to the suffering created by violence can be seen most clearly in the limited but ongoing counseling that pastors engage in with woman abuse survivors. The two situations clergy are called upon to deal with most often are "a woman with an abusive partner" or "a woman who was abused in childhood by a parent." While a small proportion of ministers report substantial experience in this area, the average pastor spends two afternoons a week providing some form of relationship counseling (Nason-Clark, 1997). Many religious women do seek out their church leaders when their experience of family life deviates from the Christian ideal of marital and family bliss.

But what advice are they offered within the confines of pastoral counseling? Clergy are more likely to interpret a husband's verbal abuse toward his partner as a marital problem of poor communication skills and to underestimate the economic and social dependency that a married woman experiences (Nason-Clark, 1999). While clergy are often slow to recognize a husband's abuse of power within the confines of marriage, or to name such behavior as woman abuse, clergy are decisive in their explicit condemnation of violent behavior on the part of a man toward either his wife or his children. Moreover, most clergy recognize that they are rather poorly equipped to respond to the needs of abuse victims and their families. The ongoing training needs of clergy have not been fully addressed by denominational offices, in part a result of very modest staff and monetary resources.

Evangelical clergy who want to make their churches a safe place to disclose violence need to: (a) recognize that abuse exists in church families, as well as in the neighborhoods where churches serve; (b) identify the unique role of the pastoral counselor; (c) ensure that victimized religious women are offered choices in their journey from victim to survivor; (d) support violence-free family living from the sacred pulpit to the relaxed church picnic; and (e) build bridges to the community so that collaborative relationships can be developed between religious and secular caregivers responding to woman abuse in their local area (Nason-Clark, 1998).

Because most church women have received help from another woman in the church at some time in their lives, the religious women in our sample understood what it meant to be both a "caregiver" and a "care receiver." Thus, women's emotional support and empowerment for one another is practiced on an ongoing basis within the weekly routine of evangelical church life. It serves to reinforce the importance of faith, and it offers women a vehicle by which to demonstrate to others their love of Christ and their love of "the sisters." Because most women have been the recipient of another woman's care, there is no embarrassment or anxiety associated with this woman-centered form of support. While church women report that they are impatient with the slow pace of movement on wife battery by their clerical leaders (Nason-Clark, 1995b), they are far from impatient with abuse victims who find it difficult to leave an abusive home or who return to an abusive partner after having received supportive services from either a transition house or a church (Beaman and Nason-Clark, 1997a). The support circle encompasses women within the evangelical church, but it is not limited to only "sisters in the faith." In fact, the strongest link between the local secular transition house and contemporary churches is forged by groups of church women who seek to translate their religious ideology into supportive services for these shelters, such as gifts of time, goods, or money (Beaman and Nason-Clark, 1997b).

In sum, our research program involving more than 600 evangelical ministers and church women has revealed that abused religious women do look to their churches for help when their family life fails to offer them safety and security. While most pastors feel inadequately prepared to meet the counseling demands of woman abuse victims, they do not turn women away, nor do they advise them to remain indefinitely in a home where their physical or mental health is put at risk. Yet the most obvious source of support for an abused religious woman is the support circle of other women of shared faith who listen to her needs and walk alongside her on the road to healing and recovery.

Defining the Difference: Reconciliation

One of the major criticisms leveled against conservative Protestantism's response to violence against women is its emphasis on reconciliation, often with little or no understanding of the dynamics of abusive relationships. Christian writing, while condemning wife abuse, also presents strategies for bringing the abuser and the victim together in a "whole" family relationship (cf. Alsdurf and Alsdurf, 1989). In this process of reconciliation, women are often called upon to offer sacrificial love to the abuser to facilitate healing. Do evangelical women accept the rhetoric of reconciliation and forgiveness? Based on the interviews with this group of women, we must answer a qualified yes.

In their haste to preserve the marital relationship, not all women responded to victims of abuse with appropriate advice or intervention, as is reflected in this woman's comment:

> This one woman in particular who was thinking of leaving her husband, I prayed with her and asked her to try and hang in there, and I think one of the things that I remember her saying was that she was really pleased at my suggestion…that she try and think of things that would be his favorites—you know, like do some extra things for him…well, they are still together. (#72, age 48)

Though this type of response is not common, it does reveal the fact that not all evangelical women are aware of the nature of abusive relationships, and that the desire to keep the marriage together may obscure victims' needs. The tendency to emphasize reconciliation is reflected in this woman's advice:

> [B]eing a Christian, I would not, unless he is physically abusing her, I would not recommend she leave the home, but I wouldn't let him…I told her I wouldn't let him run all over me like that. (#51, age 52)

The emphasis on reconciliation emanates from the Christian worldview: Jesus modeled forgiveness and love, and so, too, should Christian women. The theme of reconciliation is woven throughout the interviews; though accepting of divorce as a last resort, everything should be done to restore the relationship. Reflecting the primacy of the mothering role, evangelical women were often likely to support marriage breakdown and abandon notions of reconciliation if they perceived that children were being harmed by the continuation of a marital relationship. Perhaps rooted in their belief in the life-changing power of a Christian commitment, evangelical women believe that change is possible. Therefore, they may be more willing to invest time and energy to repair a broken relationship. The emphasis on reconciliation should not be viewed as a willingness to abandon a victim to an abusive marriage. For evangelical women, implicit in the desirability of reconciliation is the understanding that the abuse must stop.

What is interesting about the responses of evangelical women in this study is that their woman-centered practice and definitions of abuse are situated in the context of a community that does not readily embrace feminism. The complex issue of women's difference is manifested among evangelical women in that the establishment and continuance of women-only organizations, while imposed by a patriarchal structure (the same one that denies women positions of leadership in the church), has also provided unique opportunities for women to provide support, or to minister, to other women, both within the faith community and the secular world.[6]

Conservative Christian women's understandings are sometimes tempered by their Christian ideology. For example, they emphasize reconciliation and abuse as a family problem, but their actions in support of abused women are often "feminist." Feminist practice includes woman-centered action that provides support, resources, and empowerment to women (Kramarae and Treichler, 1992:158–60). These women, though conservative in their understandings and support of feminist ideology, are certainly engaging in feminist practice in relation to the issue of wife abuse.

There are, however, two major distinctions between the activities of evangelical women in relation to wife abuse and those of their secular counterparts. First, evangelicals offer local solutions to individual problems. The actions of evangelical women are not, in this context, politically motivated, nor do they link the "personal with the political," except in their explanations for abuse. Second, there is a tendency to emphasize reconciliation as a solution for individual couples. However, like their secular sisters, evangelical women focus on the practical needs of abused women who seek their help.

---

[6]For a discussion of the YWCA, see Pederson (1995).

Evangelical women emphasize practical aspects of support in their response to abused women, while combining them with sacred responses such as prayer for and with victims of abuse. It may be that abuse represents a breach in the plausibility structure of the conservative Protestant worldview. Church and biblical responses to abuse have not adequately recognized the realities of the needs of abused women, and therefore both in their understandings of and responses to violence against women, evangelical Christians import secular explanations and responses, particularly those that are woman-centered.

The Abused Christian Woman

Although the purpose of this study was not to measure the incidence of violence among evangelical families, one of the goals of the research was to gain at least a preliminary understanding of how abused Christian women understand their own pain and suffering. How does their evangelical worldview impact on their understandings of abuse? Do they think they have a duty to submit to abuse? How have they "managed" the abusive relationship? The following discussion offers some brief exploratory insights into the lives of a small group of abused Christian women, based on the stories of ten women (of the ninety-four participants) who disclosed that they were currently living in abusive relationships. Of their husbands, only two were described as Christian. The abuse the women suffered ranged from physical to emotional abuse. Their strategies for dealing with the abuse varied.

One woman used her local transition house as a way to take time out from her abusive relationship, but combined this worldly solution with prayer. She reported that her own Christian commitment is an important source of strength in her life.

> He [God] gives me all the strength that I need to get through, and like, and I pray, quite a bit, like especially, at the time, say if my husband was mentally abusing me, okay, then I tried to discipline myself to start praying for him. And that was it keeps my…it keeps my mouth shut, because if…if…like I say, if you start…saying things back, it's just going to get worse. (#71, age 42)

While most women report that their faith communities are important resources in dealing with abusive relationships, this is not always the case. One woman spoke bitterly about the lack of support and understanding within her church. This bitterness does not, however, carry over into her relationship with God. The tension between their lived experiences and the Christian model for marriage is eased somewhat by their optimism that their husbands will share their worldview. The small group of abused women interviewed in this study viewed themselves not as suffering servants, but as active agents in the process of the negotiation of day-to-day life.

It is perhaps this group of women that poses the greatest challenge in terms of making sense of their decisions. It would be easy to dismiss them as deluded victims whose religion binds them to an oppressive and dangerous ideal of marital relationships. Yet we know that most abused women, Christian or not, cling to an ideal of relationships and the hope that "he will change." Martha Mahoney offers an interesting interpretive framework for thinking about abused women in terms other than suffering servants who have sacrificed their agency and autonomy to an illusive Christian ideal. Mahoney argues that the dichotomization of women's experiences into "victim" or "agent" obscures the realities of women's lives (1994). If we dismiss a woman's self-descriptions of being in control as "false consciousness," we deny her agency and force her into the role of victim, even when she refuses to describe herself that way. Acknowledging the possibility that agency and oppression can exist simultaneously allows for a more textured understanding of the lives of abused women, which reflects their descriptions of themselves. Such a conceptualization also allows for diversity of experience among abused women. For the women who participated in this study, both agency and oppression were part of their experiences of living with abusive husbands. One caveat is that the acknowledgment of agency/oppression is *not* an acceptance of abuse in relationships and should not be construed in that way.

Like many of my evangelical clients when I practiced law, the abused women in this study often sought information and services that helped them to maneuver in their abusive relationships—they had been to lawyers, transition houses, and social service agencies. Though I was at first frustrated by my clients' decisions to remain in abusive relationships, I eventually came to see that, like the women represented in the case studies, they were simply gathering tools with which they could better handle their marital relationships.[7] They used interventions like staying at their local transition house at times when they knew it would have the most impact on their abusers. I came to appreciate their resourcefulness and to recognize them as agents, not simply as victims.

Clearly the glorification of suffering as part of the Christian story has implications for abused women. Some see their suffering as a direct result of their disobedience to God. Such self-blame is not limited to Christian women, however. To some extent all abused women blame themselves and their choices or behaviors for their own suffering. Christianity provides one framework used by women to make sense of their lives. Feminist theologians such as Bohn and Brown (1989) have examined the relationship between abuse and Christianity in detail. They argue that the notion of a punitive God must be replaced if abused Christian women are to find resources for healing within the Christian church.

Conclusions

Explorations of the links between church teachings, such as the glorification of suffering, and woman abuse need to be more fully developed if we are to understand how churches can better respond to the needs of abused women within their congregations. This chapter has given a glimpse into how abused Christian women make sense of their suffering, and how, in the context of an abusive relationship, they draw strength from their Christian commitment. For abused Christian women, an evangelical worldview is both liberating and life-giving, while at the same time exacerbating the tendency to blame one's own actions as justification for the abuse being suffered.

From the perspective of evangelical women, their faith is seen not as a liability, but as an asset that has helped them to get through situations with which they might not otherwise have found the strength to cope. They make sense of their situations by seeing them as an impetus to commit their lives to Christ, or as teaching them a lesson that will help them to reach out to others. While they have used secular resources, their Christian communities and friends are of central importance to them. For the most part, these women see themselves as fully competent agents who have made

---

[7]Whipple (1987) argues that secular counselors need to employ special strategies when helping battered women from fundamentalist churches.

choices that are for the benefit of themselves and their families. Paradoxically, while God is in control, they take responsibility for their actions and decisions.

The issue of violence against women is one that resonates personally for many women, no matter what their religious conviction. This chapter has explored a number of issues related to the complex interconnections between some of the rhetoric of evangelical Christianity, the experiences of evangelical women, and the mediating effects of secular ideologies as they impact on the response of conservative Protestant women to the suffering of abused women with whom they have contact. Can we describe their response as activism? Certainly they do not categorize it in such a manner. For some women, their response is rooted in a larger goal to end violence against women. For others, attempting to meet the needs of victims of abuse is simply a response to a fellow human being in pain and in need. In defining and explaining abuse, evangelical women use both secular and sacred tools to construct a framework in which they can understand and respond to violence against women.

8

Agency and Ideology

The discussion in the previous chapters raises some broader sociological issues. How do we assess belief systems? Is it even appropriate to describe the evangelical worldview as a belief system? We know that evangelical women appropriate secular ideas and incorporate them into their personal worldview. Belief systems are sometimes dismissed as "ideology." What does it mean to talk about ideology? Is one belief system right and another wrong? If not, how do we make basic distinctions between what is right and wrong, or what is emancipatory and what is oppressive? Are evangelical women mere dupes in the evangelical web of ideology? Is there some greater "truth" about their own emancipation that becomes obscured by their religious worldview? Does their Christian commitment mean that they remain the victims of patriarchy?

Ideology and False Consciousness

The problem of the meaning of ideology has a long history in the social sciences. Abercrombie et al. state that "[it] is widely agreed that the notion of ideology has given rise to more analytical and conceptual difficulties than almost any other term in the social sciences" (1980:187). They set out two basic approaches to the term: The first is to understand ideology as referring to "distinctive *kinds* of belief which are produced by particular social structures"

(1980:187). As Abercrombie et al. point out, inherent in this approach is an understanding that the produced beliefs are "false" or "partisan" beliefs. The second approach is to use the term to refer to "any set of beliefs regardless of its social causation of its truth or falsity" (1980:186). In this book I have used the term *ideology* in the latter sense, although I am well aware of the fact that in the analysis of conservative religious movements, the tendency has been to use it in the former sense (Kaufman, 1991; Ammerman, 1987).

While the most vigorous debate over the meaning of ideology has arisen in the context of understanding of the works of Marx and Engels, other forums have yielded similar discussions as well. For example, within religious discourse there is dissension over ideology, a conflict that has manifested itself as "Baptist battles" (Ammerman, 1990) and, on a larger scale, as "culture wars" (Hunter, 1991). Ammerman records the fight for control over the Southern Baptist Convention, a battle that is rooted in disputes over ideology, and more particularly, between "liberal" and "conservative" factions of the Convention. Hunter maps a broader-scale culture war between groups that he labels "cultural conservatives" and "progressives." Questions about "truth" and "false consciousness" have also arisen in the context of feminism and conservative Protestantism, sometimes in subtle ways.[1]

Abercrombie et al. succinctly summarize the relationship between ideology and agency:

> If a theory has a strong view of the efficacy of cultural symbols, in either causal or hermeneutic terms, as influencing or directing behavior, then the human agency either disappears or becomes merely the carrier or recipient of ideological messages. The human agent is converted into a *tabula rasa* on which the media inscribe messages. The stronger the theory of ideology, the weaker the agent. (1990:248).

In the previous pages I have explored in some detail the balance between ideology and agency as found in a particular "social world" or "milieu." The evangelical women I interviewed are neither blank slates nor, to use their own word, "doormats."

---

[1]For example, in the index of their book *Women, Men and Society*, Claire Renzetti and Daniel Curran list under ideology the subjects of "religion" and "work roles." Why did they not list feminisms under ideology? Is religion, as ideology, possibly a false consciousness and feminism not?

For Marx and Engels, ideologies are dangerous because, though as a set of beliefs they purport to explain the world, they are also rooted in class relationships, and as such are a means by which hegemony is preserved (Bryson, 1992:78). An extended application of the Marxist theory of ideology moves beyond class to consider interests other than purely economic ones. We might say of evangelicalism that it is an ideology rooted in patriarchy or sexist gender relations, and that as such it serves to preserve unequal power relations between men and women. In this view, conservative Protestant ideology works to mask women's true potential and their real experiences (for example, their satisfaction with involvement in the paid labor force). As an opiate, evangelical ideology causes women to be lulled into the belief that they are happy, masking the real oppression and exploitation they suffer. In this way their adherence to evangelical ideology creates a false consciousness.

But ideologies are also seen to contain an element of truth, albeit, in the view of some theorists, a distorted truth (Bryson, 1992:78). This is in fact the power of ideologies—they resonate existentially with those who adhere to them. Susan Boyd points out that it is important that ideologies reflect life experiences. She says that "while this element is what makes many ideologies so powerful, it does not necessarily mean that ideologies either reflect or distort 'true experience'" (1991:97). She argues that when experience conflicts with ideology, discourses that counter that ideology are more likely to emerge (ibid.). As we have already seen, evangelical women reshape the doctrine of submission so that it "makes sense" to them in their everyday lives. By interpreting it to include mutuality and partnership, submission can become a vehicle for equality, rather than simply perpetuating inferiority and powerlessness.

If we compare the actions of secular feminists and evangelical women, we can see that although woman-centered action certainly exists among evangelical women, it is not politicized in the same way that such action is in the feminist community. In addition, some feminisms are separatist, a position clearly not tenable within the evangelical community. While the two ideologies have many distinctive characteristics, there are points of interdependence and commonality that emerge, the emphasis on mothering being but one example. Though these ideologies are often at odds (at least on the surface), they cannot be separated as if they were completely distinct.

As I have argued throughout this book, evangelical ideology is not worked out in the same way by all conservative Protestant women. For example, for some of the participants in this study, evangelism means proselytizing door-to-door; for others, it translates into leading a life that exemplifies service, which can be held up as an example of God's love. The women who participated in this study emphasized various aspects of evangelical ideology. A similar comment can be made about feminist thought and practice, in which ideological variations abound. As agents, women interpret and act on diverse ideological commitments in a variety of ways.

In each other's eyes, feminists and evangelical Christians are clinging to ideologies that represent a false consciousness. Evangelical women often view feminism as the antithesis of Christianity in that it promotes a self-centered life rather than one that is devoted to the service of Jesus and to others. Feminists, on the other hand, sometimes see evangelical Christian women as doormats, who follow ideology that can only promote their inequality and reinforce the patriarchal order feminism seeks to destroy. What these two groups do share is their commitment to a cause—for feminism it is women's equality, and for evangelical women it is Christ. Yet these are not mutually exclusive aims. Evangelical women themselves point out that Christ treated women as equals and modeled a love of all humans, regardless of gender, race, ability, or age.

The debate around false consciousness is less than productive and is one that can be pursued with no real resolution. Kaufman explores the false consciousness criticism as it is directed at Orthodox Jewish women. She argues that such accusations fail to grasp that "women are often simultaneously victims and agents, subjects and object. Theoretical categories cannot distinguish between an 'authentic' and an 'alienated' woman's experience. Vital human experiences cannot be reduced to abstract orthodoxies—feminist or religious" (1991:68).[2] Given the fruitlessness of the false consciousness debate, perhaps it is time we abandoned the notion of a "truth" against which sets of beliefs are measured and pronounced "false."[3]

---

[2]In addition, such criticisms ignore the long history of biblical criticism by Christian women who have sought to reinterpret the Bible in ways that eliminate patriarchal interpretations (see Lerner, 1993).

[3]The development of alternative notions of truth has been one of the results of postmodernism. This in turn raises the thorny issue of relativism (see Nicholson, 1990). For one discussion of the problem of relativism, see Bryant (1996).

Ideology, Practice, and Agency

The experiences and beliefs of the women who participated in this study illustrate how evangelical women translate evangelical ideology in a manner that corresponds with their experiences. There is an evangelical ideology, the hallmark of which is the ideal of service, or an other-centered focus. However, evangelical women are uncomfortable describing themselves as "activists," a term that, for them, conjures up images of extremism. Conservative Protestant culture both calls and allows women to highlight their mothering role. Evangelical women see themselves as different from those in the secular world, thus their daily activities incorporate, in addition to religious practices such as prayer and devotions, simple boundary markers such as the type of television programming they watch, the books they read, and the friends with whom they associate. Routines center around church activities such as prayer groups, Bible studies, choir, children's ministries, and church services. In the course of day-to-day living, evangelical women combine a rhetoric of choice with a rhetoric of duty and obligation. They reference a model of Christian living in determining how to behave as good Christians, yet they preserve for themselves the freedom to choose within this model.

Despite their early historical participation in the feminist movement, evangelical women are not entirely comfortable with present-day feminism. However, although they are cautious and sceptical regarding some of the rhetoric of feminism, evangelical women do support many of the goals of feminism, and indeed, many of the women who participated in this study actually described themselves as feminists. Resistant to what they perceive as a militant strain within feminism, evangelical women are nonetheless supportive of liberal feminist goals like pay equity and equal employment opportunities for women. Combining evangelical ideology and feminist ideology is viewed as possible, but only if one's Christian commitment takes precedence. One of the primary links between evangelical women and feminism is an emphasis on women as "different," particularly in their role as mothers.

A number of themes have emerged from the data presented in the preceding chapters that highlight the ways in which evangelical women interpret evangelical ideology in their daily lives. First, evangelical women are not a monolithic group; they interpret ideology in diverse ways, and they represent a variety of life experiences. Second, the view of evangelicalism from the outside is quite different than the view from the inside; in setting aside preconceived notions and judgments, we can begin to understand how evangelical women themselves interpret evangelical ideology in sometimes surprising ways. Third, in the process of interpreting evangelical ideology, conservative Protestant women negotiate boundaries between their sacred world and secular culture. Finally, despite their commitment to an ideology that perpetuates patriarchy, it is clear that evangelical women perceive themselves as agents, not doormats.

Diversity

Like any group of people who subscribe to a common ideology, evangelical women are diverse. Although the women in this study are guided by conservative Protestant ideology, they are not monolithic in their response to it. Participants can be roughly divided into three basic groups: "traditionalists," "moderates," and "liberals." The first is that group of women who are very traditional in their approach to women's roles and more literal in their interpretation of biblical prescriptions. This group might be characterized as fundamentalist (although only one participant actually used that word to describe herself). The second group, who make up the majority of the participants, are more moderate in their approach. They are less likely to subscribe to headship and submission without qualification, and they express a greater willingness to embrace feminism, though they are careful to delineate what they could not reconcile with their Christian commitment. The third group is more liberal in its interpretations of evangelical ideology. They are more likely to reject notions of headship and submission, seeing the Christian marriage as a partnership with no need for lip service to those evangelical doctrines that can be interpreted to diminish women's equality. This group of women are also more likely to call themselves Christian feminists. These categories are loose and intended only as a broad characterization: For example, not all women who reject submission call themselves Christian feminists. The point is that evangelical Christian women range from those who adhere to a traditionalist stance to those who are somewhat liberal in their interpretations of evangelical doctrines; each woman considered herself to be an evangelical Christian. While each of these responses could be characterized as "evangelical" and thus fall within conservative Protestant ideology, they are, clearly, diverse. Like the diversity to be found among feminists, evangelical women translate evangelical ideology in ways that help them to make sense of their own experiences as mothers, wives, volunteers, and members of the paid labor force.

The View from Inside

As Kaufman notes, the first step in trying to understand a group of people is to explore their world from their point of view: Once inside, things often seem quite different, and new understanding emerges. Of course, the task of the sociologist is to transcend merely reporting the inside, to offer an analysis of the group or phenomenon. However, getting the view from the inside is the first crucial step. Kaufman argues that in sociological analysis it is important to suspend preconceived judgments and assessments (1991:3). This study has explored the evangelical worldview from the inside—how do evangelical women see themselves, how do they understand their lives as being different from those who do not ascribe to a conservative Protestant worldview?

From the outside, evangelical Christians are sometimes perceived as being closed-minded extremists who are intent on "converting" at any cost (Ammerman, 1987). Interestingly, this is the image that evangelical women report trying to avoid. Aversion to extremism was a theme that emerged in their own definitions of what it means to be an evangelical and again in their discussions of feminism. Perhaps the aspect of the data that revealed most sharply the disjuncture between insider and outsider viewpoints is the discussion of submission. Much of the evangelical rhetoric surrounding submission is reproduced with little examination of how evangelical women themselves understand, experience, and operationalize this doctrine. By exploring the perspectives of evangelical women, we gain insight into the ways in which they interpret the dogma of submission in the context of their everyday lives.

Their discussion of feminism also illuminates insider–outsider differences. Similar to some feminists' perceptions of evangelicalism, conservative Protestant women often have a limited understanding of feminism based, it seems, primarily on the narrow perspective of feminism presented by the media, and, perhaps, by the leaders in their churches. However, contrary to what might have been expected, they are not hostile to feminist ideology, and in fact embrace aspects that help them to make sense of their own experiences. They are similar to difference feminists in their celebration of the "unique" nature of women. In addition, they incorporate feminist theories of violence in their understanding of woman abuse. Their support of transition houses, which are traditionally firmly rooted in the feminist community, is also an indication of the insights an "insider" exploration can provide.

Boundary Negotiation

A key to the preservation of ideology is the commitment by those who ascribe to it to perpetuate it through their daily activities (Ammerman, 1987; Kraybill, 1989). Indeed, this is central to the evangelical way of life: Participants often mentioned behaviors that they feared might "mar their witness." In the process of living out ideology, adherents create, maintain, and negotiate boundaries. For evangelicals, these boundaries take a variety of forms: through their material culture, such as Bible cozies, wall hangings with Bible verses, a particular style of home decorating—visible markers that make a statement about their ideological commitment. Such boundaries not only declare that "we are different," but also signal to other evangelicals that "we are one of you."

Boundaries are also established through lifestyle, including holiness practices, such as abstention from alcohol. Participants in this study also "mark the boundaries" through the books they read, the television programs they watch, and the friends they have. Declarations of difference are manifested in many women through an almost total immersion in evangelical culture—their daily activities are integrally linked to their faith communities. The evangelicals in this study clearly view themselves as different. In their marriages, they see themselves as being committed for life, unlike those in the secular world, who are viewed as being prone to divorce. In their attitudes, they strive to think of others first and to demonstrate that commitment through daily acts of kindness and generosity. They lament the attitude of self-centeredness that to them seems to pervade the secular world. In their demonstration of a selfless attitude, evangelical women create boundaries between themselves and those who do not share their faith commitment.

The tendency to think of themselves as different and the need to preserve boundaries between themselves and secular society has an important impact on how evangelical women think about violence in the home. Though they use secular explanations to understand violence against women generally, when pressed to interpret the existence of violence in Christian homes, they turn to sacred explanations. Further, the pressure to be different and the resulting concern about image may have the effect of suppressing the reporting of problems in Christian families. Women, in particular, feel the need to present a "happy face." There is a tension between the lived experiences of women and the ideal Christian family. The reality is sometimes obscured by the desire to present the ideal. Why focus on boundaries and difference? Evangelical Christians believe that a commitment to Christ fundamentally alters one's life. By declaring boundaries and defending their difference from the secular world, conservative Protestants both preserve their culture and demonstrate that a Christian commitment does make a difference.

Women as Agents

Throughout the preceding chapters we have seen how evangelical women interpret and mediate conservative Protestant ideology based on their own experiences. As evangelicals, they are called to share the "word," a task that the women who participated in this study shape as a daily commitment to witnessing through their everyday lives. Though sometimes not comfortable verbalizing their Christian commitment, evangelical women model a Christian way of life through an emphasis on service. Service in this context often includes reaching out to other women in need.

Perhaps the most controversial aspect of evangelical ideology in relation to the agency of women is the doctrine of submission. Yet we do need to understand women's agency as occurring within oppressive contexts. The denial of positions of leadership for women, the emphasis on mothering and nurturing as women's "true" calling, and the promotion of a hierarchical view of family life are certainly *indicia* of patriarchy, but they do not preclude the possibility of women's agency. Further, evangelical women reshape conservative Protestant dogma in ways that facilitate their own equality. Thus, for example, they interpret submission as mutual submission, and they see themselves as equal partners in their marital relationships. In some ways, evangelical women may be seen to be subverting or diffusing the dogma of submission through their emphasis on the mothering role: They place priority on their relationships with their children, not their husbands.

Conclusion

How can we understand women's agency so as to avoid a relativist stance that evades a commitment to any one set of values? How can we choose a stance that honors the experiences and beliefs of women while at the same time supports women's equality? Both evangelical women and feminists are too quick to leap to conclusions about each other. Unfortunately, each group seems to accept media portrayals of the extremes of the other, excluding the possibility that there is much common ground. While admittedly there are likely to be points of tension, especially at the extremes, we must remember that the extremes represent a minority of women.

Recognizing the possibility of agency within oppressive contexts is key to understanding and acknowledging the complexities of women's lives. A necessary beginning place for any exploration of women's agency is with a view from the inside. By examining how women themselves see their lives, it is then possible to reflect on agency and equality in a manner that is not dismissive of women's experiences and worldviews. Gaining an insider's view forces one to engage with the position of the "other." Agency and oppression are not mutually exclusive: Acknowledging agency does not necessitate denying oppression. Evangelical women are empowered through their beliefs and through their connectedness to their faith communities. They do live submission as partnership in their everyday lives. But they also are excluded from clerical leadership positions and from control over the coffers of their churches. The story then becomes one about the ways in which evangelical women exercise agency within a religious context that promotes patriarchal relations.

Although both prescriptive and explanatory, evangelical ideology is not operationalized monolithically; rather it is shaped by women, reflecting their diverse life experiences. Through the process of interpretation, evangelical women exercise agency:

They are not doormats, but active agents who rework ideology as a source of empowerment, rather than oppressive dogma. Despite their reinterpretation of evangelical ideology, the women who participated in this study do see themselves as different from their secular counterparts. Evangelical women construct and maintain boundaries between these two worlds through their everyday activities. They are anxious to distinguish their marriages, the way they raise their children, their beliefs, and their lifestyles from what they perceive to be the self-centeredness of secular society. In maintaining these boundaries, evangelical women demonstrate that they are, indeed, different.

Appendix:

The Methodology of This Study

Although they shared similar beliefs, the women who participated in this study held a broad variety of perspectives on the role of women in society, the church, and the family. To gain a clearer understanding of their perspective on their similarities and their differences, categories were constructed that were modeled after those used by Lyn Gesch in her study of women in mainstream religion (1995). Gesch's work provided a useful guideline in establishing meaningful groupings. She states that "conceptually, an egalitarian role orientation is one that stresses equality and similarity in the roles of men and women, while a traditional orientation stresses the difference between roles for men and women, with women's lives centered on home and family" (1995:126). She categorized respondents using an index of four items from the 1988 General Statistical Survey. They were: (1) A working mother can establish just as warm a relationship with her children as a woman who does not work; (2) It is more important for a wife to help her husband's career than to have one herself; (3) A preschool child is likely to suffer if her/his mother works; (4) It is better if the man is the achiever outside the home and the woman takes care of the home and family. Gesch placed each female respondent in one of three categories based on their responses. Those who disagreed on question 1 and agreed on 2, 3, and 4 were labeled "traditional," while those who agreed on 1 and disagreed on 2, 3, and 4 were labeled "feminist." Those scoring in any other combination were labeled "moderate" as their responses did not lean consistently in one direction. In her analysis, Gesch focused on only the two extreme groups for the purpose of comparison. She found that religiosity and gender-role orientation were connected, in that traditional women were more conventional in their religious beliefs and involvement, while feminists were less conventional and more individualistic (1995:126). In adapting these categories for use with the data gathered from interviews with evangelical women, both quantitative and qualitative data was available. Each interview consisted of both in-depth, open-ended questions and a set of scale questions. One scale focused specifically on gender roles and required the interviewee to respond to a set of statements with one of four options: strongly agree, agree, disagree, or strongly disagree. Five items were selected from this scale to create an index similar to the one used by Lyn Gesch: (1) A mother's main responsibility is in the home; (2) The responsibility of the husband is to be the primary breadwinner; (3) Women with preschool children should be full-time homemakers; (4) Wives should seek paid employment only when it is financially necessary; (5) Care of children should be primarily in the hands of women. Similar to Gesch's method, a scoring guide was implemented that ensured that the traditional and feminist categories included only those respondents who answered consistently in one direction.

The five items that were selected were all "traditionally" oriented. Responses of "agree" or "strongly agree" on an item were scored as 1 and responses of "disagree" or "strongly disagree" were scored as 2. Therefore, a consistent traditional response on all five items equals a score of 5, and consistent feminist responses score 10. Any scores ranging from 6–9 were labeled moderate because the opinion of these respondents falls between the two extremes. Each respondent was initially assigned to one of these categories. For instance, a respondent who scored as "Feminist" on the scale questions may have expressed some more tentative or even traditional views when examined more deeply; however, this was not a final assessment but rather a tentative placement based on only a small portion of the data. Upon reading through each woman's open-ended responses and drawing out responses to illustrate their point of view, further evidence sometimes suggested that they should be categorized as a more deeply held opinion, indicating a better fit in the moderate category.

Selected References

Abercrombie, Nicholas, Stephen Hill, and Bryan S. Turner
  1980   *The Dominant Ideology Thesis*. London: Allen and Unwin.
  1990   *Dominant Ideologies*. London: Unwin Hyman.

Abrahamson, Mark
  1983   *Social Research Methods*. Englewood Cliffs, N.J.: Prentice-
          Hall.

Alsdurf, James, and Phyllis Alsdurf
  1989   *Battered into Submission: The Tragedy of Wife Abuse in the
          Christian Home*. Naperville, Ill.: InterVarsity Press.

Alumkal, Antony
  1994   "Small Groups in a Campus Ministry: Shaping the
          Future." In *'I Come Away Stronger': How Small Groups are
          Shaping American Religion*, 251–74. Edited by Robert
          Wuthnow. Grand Rapids, Mich.: Eerdmans.

Ammerman, Nancy Tatom
  1987   *Bible Believers: Fundamentalists in the Modern World*. New
          Brunswick, N.J.: Rutgers University Press.
  1990   *Baptist Battles: Social Change and Religious Conflict in the
          Southern Baptist Convention*. New Brunswick, N.J.: Rutgers
          University Press.
  1997   "Organized Religion in a Voluntaristic Society." *Sociology of
          Religion* 58 (3): 203–15.

Anderson, Margaret L.
  1993   *Thinking About Women: Sociological Perspectives on Sex and
          Gender*. New York: Macmillan.

Balmer, Randall
  1994   "American Fundamentalism: The Ideal of Femininity." In
          Fundamentalism and Gender. Edited by John Stratton
          Hawley. New York: Oxford University Press.

Banks, Olive
  1986   *Faces of Feminism*. Oxford: Basil Blackwell.

Beaman, Lori G.
  1997   "Collaborators or Resistors?: Evangelical Women in
          Atlantic Canada." *Atlantis* 22 (1): 9–18.

Beaman-Hall, Lori G.
  1994   "Too Heavenly Minded to be Any Earthly Good? Religious
          Responses to Wife Abuse as Evidenced by a
          Denominational Publication." Paper presented at the
          annual meetings of the Canadian Sociology and
          Anthropology Association in Calgary, Alberta.

Beaman, Lori G., and Nancy Nason-Clark
   1997a   "Partners or Protagonists: Exploring the Relationship
           between the Transition House Movement and
           Conservative Churches." *Affilia* 12 (2): 176–96.
   1997b   "Translating Spiritual Commitment into Service: The
           Response of Evangelical Women to Wife Abuse." *Canadian
           Journal of Women's Studies* 17 (Winter, 1): 58–61.

Bendroth, Margaret Lamberts
   1993   *Fundamentalism and Gender, 1875 to the Present.* New Haven,
           Conn.: Yale University Press.

Berger, Peter
   1969   *The Sacred Canopy: Elements of a Sociological Theory of
           Religion.* New York: Anchor Books.

Bibby, Reginald
   1987   *Fragmented Gods: The Poverty and Potential of Religion in
           Canada.* Toronto: Irwin.
   1993   *Unknown Gods: The Ongoing Story of Religion in Canada.*
           Toronto: Irwin.
   1995   *EvangelTrends.* A Summary Report Prepared for the Vision
           2000 Canada 1995 Consultations on Evangelism, Waterloo,
           Ont.: Vision 2000 Canada.

Bineham, Jeffery L.
   1993   "Theological Hegemony and Oppositional Interpretive
           Codes: The Case of Evangelical Christian Feminism."
           Western Journal of Communication 57: 515–29.

Bohn, Carole R.
   1989   "Dominion to Rule: The Roots and Consequences of a
           Theology of Ownership." In *Christianity, Patriarchy and
           Abuse: A Feminist Critique*, 105–16. Edited by Joanne
           Carlson Brown and Carole R. Bohn. Cleveland, Ohio:
           Pilgrim Press.

Bordo, Susan
   1990   "Feminism, Postmodernism, and Gender-Scepticism." In
           Feminism/Postmodernism, 133–56. Edited by Linda J.
           Nicholson. New York: Routledge.

Boyd, Susan
   1991   "Some Postmodernist Challenges to Feminist Analyses of
           Law, Family, and State: Ideology and Discourse in Child
           Custody Law." *Canadian Journal of Family Law* 10: 79–113.

Brasher, Brenda E.
   1997   "My Beloved is All Radiant: Two Case Studies of
           Congregational-Based Christian Fundamentalist Female

Enclaves and the Religious Experiences They Cultivate Among Women." *Review of Religious Research* 38 (3): 231–46.

1998   *Godly Women: Fundamentalism and Female Power.* New Brunswick, N.J.: Rutgers University Press.

Brown, David, and Judith Kulig

1998   "The Concept of Resiliency: Theoretical Lessons from Community Research." *Health and Canadian Society* 4 (1): 29–50.

Brown, Joanne Carlson, and Rebecca Parker

1989   "For God So Loved the World?" In *Christianity, Patriarchy, and Abuse: A Feminist Critique*, 1–30. Edited by Joanne Carlson Brown and Carole R. Bohn. Cleveland: Pilgrim Press.

Brown, Karen McCarthy

1994   "Fundamentalism and the Control of Women." In *Fundamentalism and Gender*, 175–201. Edited by John Stratton Hawley. New York: Oxford University Press.

Bryant, Joseph M.

1996   *Moral Codes and Social Structure in Ancient Greece: A Sociology of Greek Ethics from Homer to the Epicureans and Stoics.* Albany, N.Y.: SUNY Press.

Bryson, Valerie

1992   *Feminist Political Theory: An Introduction.* London: Macmillan.

Burns, Gene

1996   "Studying the Political Culture of American Catholicism." *Sociology of Religion* 57 (1): 37–53.

Bussert, Joy M. K.

1986   *Battered Women: From a Theology of Suffering to an Ethic of Empowerment.* Philadelphia: Division for Mission in North America, Lutheran Church in America.

Chodorow, Nancy

1992   "Family Structure and Feminine Personality." In *Feminist Philosophies: Problems, Theories, and Applications*, 309–22. Edited by Janet A. Kourany, James P. Sterba, and Rosemarie Tong. Englewood Cliffs, N.J.: Prentice-Hall.

Christ, Carol P.

1979   "Spiritual Quest and Women's Experience." In *Womanspirit Rising: A Feminist Reader in Religion*. Edited by Carol P. Christ and Judith Plaskow. San Francisco: Harper and Row.

Clegg, Stewart
    1993   "Narrative, Power, and Social Theory." In *Narrative and Social Control*, 15–45. Edited by D. K. Mumby. Thousand Oaks, Calif.: Sage.

Cohn, Steven F.
    1993   "Ministerial Power and the Iron Law and Oligarchy: A Deviant Case Analysis." *Review of Religious Research* 35 (2): 155–73.

Daly, Mary
    1968   *The Church and the Second Sex*. New York: Harper *Colophon* Books.
    1973   *Beyond God the Father: Toward a Philosophy of Women's Liberation*. Boston: Beacon Press.
    1978   *Gyn/Ecology: The Metaethics of Radical Feminism*. Boston: Beacon Press.

Davidman, Lyn
    1986   *Strength of Tradition in a Chaotic World: Women Turn to Orthodox Judaism*. Ann Arbor, Mich.: University Microfilms International.

Davis, Nancy J., and Robert V. Robinson
    1995   "Religious Orthodoxy in American Society: The Myth of a Monolithic Phalanx." Paper presented at the Annual Meetings of the Society for the Scientific Study of Religion, October 27–29, St. Louis, Missouri.

DeBerg, Betty A.
    1990   *Ungodly Women: Gender and the First Wave of American Fundamentalism*. Minneapolis: Fortress Press.

Flax, Jane
    1990   "Postmodernism and Gender Relations in Feminist Theory." In *Feminism/Postmodernism*, 39–62. Edited by Linda J. Nicholson. New York: Routledge.

Fortune, Marie
    1989   "The Transformation of Suffering: A Biblical and Theological Perspective." In *Christianity, Patriarchy, and Abuse: A Feminist Critique*, 139–47. Edited by Joanne Carlson Brown and Carole R. Bohn. Cleveland: Pilgrim Press.
    1991   *Violence in the Family: A Workshop Curriculum for Clergy and Other Helpers*. Cleveland: Pilgrim Press.

Fortune, Marie M., and Judith Hertze
    1987   "A Commentary on Religious Issues in Family Violence." In *Sexual Assault and Abuse: A Handbook for Clergy and*

Religious Professionals, 67–83. Edited by Mary Pellauer, Barbara Chester, and Jane Boyajian. San Francisco: Harper.

Fraser, Nancy, and Linda J. Nicholson
1990   "Social Criticism without Philosophy: An Encounter between Feminism and Postmodernism." In *Feminism/Postmodernism*, 19–38. Edited by Linda J. Nicholson. New York: Routledge.

Friedan, Betty
1963   *The Feminine Mystique*. New York: W. W. Norton.

Garskof, Michele Hoffnung, editor
1971   *Roles Women Play: Readings Toward Women's Liberation.* Belmont, Calif.: Brooks/Cole Publishing Company.

Gesch, Lyn
1995   "Responses to Changing Lifestyles: 'Feminists' and 'Traditionalists' in Mainstream Religion. In *Work, Family and Religion in Contemporary Society*. Edited by Nancy Tatom Ammerman and Wade Clark Roof. New York: Routledge.

Gilligan, Carol
1982   *In a Different Voice: Psychological Theory and Women's Development*. Cambridge, Mass.: Harvard University Press.

Goldenberg, Naomi R.
1979   *Changing of the Gods: Feminism and the End of Traditional Religions*. Boston: Beacon Press.

Gorham, Deborah
1976   "The Canadian Suffragists." In *Women in the Canadian Mosaic*. Edited by Gwen Matheson. Toronto: Peter Martin Associates Limited.

Greeley, Andrew
1993   "Why Catholics Stay in the Church." In *In Gods We Trust: New Patterns of Religious Pluralism in America*. Edited by Thomas Robbins and Dick Anthony, second edition. New Brunswick, N.J.: Transaction Publishers.

Griffith, R. Marie
1997   "Submissive Wives, Wounded Daughters and Female Soldiers: Prayer and Christian Womanhood in Women's Aglow Fellowship." In *Lived Religion in America*. Edited by David Hall. Princeton, N.J.: Princeton University Press.

Harding, Sandra
1987   "Is there a Feminist Method?" In *Feminism and Methodology*. Indianapolis: Indiana University Press.
1991   *Whose Science? Whose Knowledge? Thinking from Women's Lives*. Ithaca, N.Y.: Cornell University Press.

Heggen, Carolyn Holderread
1993   *Sexual Abuse in Christian Homes and Churches.* Scottdale,
        Pa.: Herald Press.

Hunter, James Davison
1987a   "The Evangelical Worldview Since 1890." In *Piety and
        Politics: Evangelicals and Fundamentalists Confront the World*,
        19–54. Edited by Richard John Neuhaus and Michael
        Cromartie. Washington, D.C.: Ethics and Public Policy
        Center.
1987b   *Evangelicalism: The Coming Generation.* Chicago: University
        of Chicago Press.
1991   *Culture Wars: The Struggle to Define America.* New York:
        Basic Books.

Jacobs, Janet Lubman
1989   *Divine Disenchantment: Deconverting from New Religions.*
        Indianapolis: Indiana University Press.

Jaggar, Alison M.
1983   *Feminist Politics and Human Nature.* New Jersey: Rowman
        and Allanhead Publishers.
1990   "Sexual Difference and Sexual Equality." In *Theoretical
        Perspectives on Sexual Difference*, 239–54. Edited by Deborah
        Rhode. New Haven, Conn.: Yale University Press.

Jelen, Ted G.
1994   Protestant Clergy as Political Leaders: Theological
        Limitations." *Review of Religious Research* 36 (1): 23–42.

Joyce, Kathleen
1994   "The Long Loneliness: Liberal Catholics and the
        Conservative Church." In *"I Come Away Stronger": How
        Small Groups are Shaping American Religion*, 55–76. Edited
        by Robert Wuthnow. Grand Rapids, Mich.: Eerdmans.

Kaufman, Debra Renee
1991   *Rachel's Daughters: Newly Orthodox Jewish Women.* New
        Brunswick, N.J.: Rutgers University Press.

Kealey, Linda
1979   *A Not Unreasonable Claim: Women and Reform in Canada in
        1880s–1920s.* Toronto: The Women's Press.

Kirby, Sandra, and Kate McKenna
1989   *Experience, Research, Social Change: Methods from the
        Margins.* Toronto: Garamond Press.

Klatch, Rebecca E.
1987   *Women of the New Right.* Philadelphia: Temple University
        Press.

Kramarae, Cheris, and Paula A. Treichler
    1992   *Amazons, Bluestockings and Crones: A Feminist Dictionary.*
            London: Pandora Press.

Kraybill, Donald B.
    1989   *The Riddle of Amish Culture.* Baltimore: Johns Hopkins
            University Press.

Kraybill, Donald B., and Marc A. Olshan, editors
    1994   *The Amish Struggle with Modernity.* Hanover, N.H.:
            University Press of New England.

LaHaye, Beverly
    1976   *The Spirit Controlled Woman.* California: Harvest House
            Publishers.

Langley, Myrtle
    1983   *Equal Women: A Christian Feminist Perspective.* Hants,
            United Kingdom: Marshalls.

Leehan, James
    1989   *Pastoral Care for Survivors of Family Abuse.* Louisville, Ky.:
            Westminster/John Knox Press.

LeGates, Marlene
    1996   *Making Waves: A History of Feminism in Western Society.*
            Toronto: Copp Clark.

Lerner, Gerda
    1986   *The Creation of Patriarchy.* New York: Oxford University
            Press.
    1993   *The Creation of Feminist Consciousness: From the Middle Ages*
            to Eighteen-Seventy. New York: Oxford University Press.

MacHaffie, Barbara J.
    1986   *Herstory: Women in Christian Tradition.* Philadelphia:
            Fortress Press.

MacKinnon, Catharine
    1989   *Towards a Feminist Theory of the State.* Cambridge, Mass.:
            Harvard University Press.

Mahoney, Martha
    1994   "Victimization or Oppression?: Women's Lives, Violence,
            and Agency." In *The Public Nature of Private Violence: The*
            Discovery of Domestic Abuse, 59–92. Edited by Martha
            Albertson Fineman and Roxanne Mykitiuk. New York:
            Routledge.

Maroney, Heather Jon
    1986   "Embracing Motherhood: New Feminist Theory." In *The*
            Politics of Diversity: Feminism, Marxism and Nationalism, 40–
            64. Edited by Roberta Hamilton and Michele Barrett.
            Montreal: Book Centre.

Marsden, George
1987   "The Evangelical Denomination." In *Piety and Politics: Evangelicals and Fundamentalists Confront the World*, 55–68. Edited by Richard John Neuhaus and Michael Cromartie. Washington, D.C.: Ethics and Public Policy Center.

Martin, Faith McBurney
1988   *Call Me Blessed: The Emerging Christian Woman*. Grand Rapids, Mich.: Eerdmans.

Martin, Sheilah L.
1991   "The Control of Women through Gender-Biased Laws on Human Reproduction." In *Feminist Legal Theory*, 22–46. Edited by Richard F. Devlin. Toronto: Edmond Montgomery Publications Limited.

Marx, Karl
1969   "Religious Illusion and the Task of History." In *Sociology and Religion: A Book of Readings*, 93–95. Edited by Norman Birnbaum and Gertrud Lenzer. Englewood Cliffs, N.J.: Prentice-Hall.

Matheson, Gwen, and V. E. Lang
1976   "Nellie McClung: 'Not a Nice Woman.'" In *Women in the Canadian Mosaic*, 1–21. Edited by Gwen Matheson. Toronto: Peter Martin Associates Limited.

McDill, S. R., and Linda McDill
1991   *Shattered and Broken*. Tarrytown, N.Y.: Fleming H. Revell Company.

Menkel-Meadow, Carrie
1992   "Mainstreaming Feminist Legal Theory." *Pacific Law Journal* 23:1493–1542.

Meyers, Carol
1988   *Discovering Eve: Ancient Israelite Women in Context*. New York: Oxford University Press.

Miles, Margaret R.
1987   "Violence Against Women in the Historical Christian West and in North American Secular Culture: The Visual and Textual Evidence." In *Shaping New Vision: Gender and Values in American Culture*, 11–29. Edited by Clarissa W. Atkinson, Constance H. Buchanan, and Margaret R. Miles. London: UMI Research Press.

Mitchinson, Wendy
1979   "The WCTU: 'For God, Home and Native Land': A Study in Nineteenth-Century Feminism." In *A Not Unreasonable Claim: Women and Reform in Canada, 1880s–1920s*. Edited by Linda Kealey. Toronto: Women's Press.

Morris, Roberta
    1988   *Ending Violence Against Families: A Training Program for Pastoral Care Workers.* Toronto: The United Church of Canada.

Nason-Clark, Nancy
    1987   "Ordaining Women as Priests: Religious vs. Sexist Explanations for Clerical Attitudes." *Sociological Analysis* 48 (3): 259–73.
    1993   "Gender Relations in Contemporary Christian Organizations." In *The Sociology of Religion: A Canadian Focus*, 215–33. Edited by W. E. Hewitt. Toronto: Butterworths.
    1995a   "Conservative Protestants and Violence Against Women: Exploring the Rhetoric and the Response." In *Sex, Lies and Sanctity: Religion and Deviance in Modern America*, 109–30. Edited by Mary Jo Neitz and Marion Goldman. Greenwich, Conn.: JAI Press.
    1995b   "Women Helping Women: Exploring Feminist Social Action Among Evangelical Women." Paper presented at the Annual Meetings of the Society for the Scientific Study of Religion, October 27–29, 1995, St. Louis, Missouri.
    1996   "Religion and Violence Against Women: Exploring the Rhetoric and the Response of Evangelical Churches in Canada." *Social Compass* 43 (4).
    1997   *The Battered Wife: How Christians Confront Family Violence.* Louisville, Ky.: Westminster John Knox Press.
    1998   "Canadian Evangelical Church Women and Responses to Family Violence," In *Religion in a Changing World*, 57–65. Edited by Madeline Gusmean. Westport: Praeger.
    1999   "Woman Abuse and Faith Communities: Religion, Violence and the Provision of Social Welfare." In *Religion and Social Policy for the 21st Century*. Edited by Paula D. Nesbitt. Walnut Creek, Calif.: AltaMira Press.

Nason-Clark, Nancy, and Lori Beaman-Hall
    1993   "Religion and Wife Abuse: Examining the Relationship Between Transition House Workers and Clergy." Paper presented at the Annual Meetings of the Society for the Scientific Study of Religion, Raleigh, N.C.
    1994   "Where are all the Christians? Understanding Evangelical Women's Responses to Church Support for Battered Women." Paper presented at the Annual Meeting of the Association for the Sociology of Religion, August 4–6, Los Angeles, California.

156 *Shared Beliefs, Different Lives*

Nason-Clark, Nancy, and Brenda Belanger
1993   "Jugglers for Jesus: Identifying Career and Family Juggling Patterns Among Conservative Religious Women." Paper presented at the Annual Meetings of the Society for the Scientific Study of Religion, Raleigh, N.C.

Neitz, Mary Jo
1987   *Charisma and Community: A Study of Religious Commitment Within the Charismatic Renewal.* New Brunswick, N.J.: Transaction Books.

Nicholson, Linda J., editor
1990   *Feminism/Postmodernism.* New York: Routledge.

Nock, David A.
1993   "The Organization of Religious Life in Canada." In *The Sociology of Religion: A Canadian Focus*, 41–62. Edited by W. E. Hewitt. Toronto: Butterworths.

Offen, Karen
1990   "Feminism and Sexual Difference in Historical Perspective." In *Theoretical Perspectives on Sexual Difference.* Edited by Deborah L. Rhode. New Haven Conn.: Yale University Press.

Olshan, Marc A., and Kimberly D. Schmidt
1994   "Amish Women and the Feminist Conundrum." In *The Amish Struggle with Modernity*, 215–30. Edited by Donald B. Kraybill and Marc A. Olshan. Hanover, N.H.: University Press of New England.

Ozorak, Elizabeth W.
1996   "The Power but not the Glory: How Women Empower Themselves Through Religion." *Journal for the Scientific Study of Religion* 35 (1): 17–29.

Palmer, Sally E., Ralph A. Brown, and Maru Barrera
1992   "Group Treatment Program for Abusive Husbands: Long Term Evaluation." *American Journal of Orthopsychiatry* 62 (1): 276–83.

Palmer, Susan
1995   *Moon Sisters, Krishna Mothers, Rajneesh Lovers: Women's Roles in New Religions.* Syracuse: Syracuse University Press.

Pape, Dorothy
1976   *God and Women: A Fresh Look at What the New Testament Says About Women.* London and Oxford: Mowbrays.

Pederson, Diana
1995   "'The Power of True Christian Women': The YWCA and Evangelical Womanhood in the Late Nineteenth Century."

In *Changing Roles of Women within the Christian Church in Canada*, 321–37. Edited by Elizabeth Gillan Muir and Marilyn Fardig Whiteley. Toronto: University of Toronto Press.

Pevey, Carolyn F.
1994   "Submission and Power among Southern Baptist Ladies." Paper presented at the Annual Meetings of the Society for the Scientific Study of Religion, Albuquerque, N.M.

Pevey, Carolyn F., Christine Williams, and Christopher Ellison
1996   "Male God Imagery and Female Submission: Lessons from a Southern Baptist Ladies' Bible Study." *Qualitative Sociology* 19 (2): 173–93.

Renzetti, Claire M., and Daniel J. Curran
1995   *Women, Men, and Society.* Boston: Allyn and Bacon.

Rhode, Deborah L.
1989   *Justice and Gender: Sex Discrimination and the Law.* Cambridge, Mass.: Harvard University Press.

Rhodes, A. Lewis
1985   "Religion and Opposition to Abortion Reconsidered." *Review of Religious Research* 27 (2): 158–68.

Roberts, Wayne
1979   "'Rocking the Cradle for the World': The New Woman and Maternal Feminism, Toronto 1877–1914." In *A Not Unreasonable Claim: Women and Reform in Canada, 1880s–1920s*, 15–45. Edited by Linda Kealey. Toronto: Women's Press.

Romanivc, Anatole
1994   "Fertility in Canada: Retrospective and Prospective." In *Perspectives on Canada's Population: An Introduction to Concepts and Issues.* Edited by Frank Trovato and Carl F. Grundstaff. Toronto: University of Toronto Press.

Rose, Susan D.
1993   "Gender, Education and the New Christian Right." In *In Gods We Trust: New Patterns of Religious Pluralism in America*, 99–117. Edited by Thomas Robbins and Dick Anthony. New Brunswick, N.J.: Transaction Books.

Rothenberg, Stuart
1987   "Evangelicals are Politically Diverse." In *Piety and Politics: Evangelicals and Fundamentalists Confront the World*, 321–26. Edited by Richard John Neuhaus and Michael Cromartie. Washington, D.C.: Ethics and Public Policy Center.

Ruddick, Sara
  1984   "Maternal Thinking." In *Mothering: Essays in Feminist
          Theory*. Edited by Joyce Treblicot. Totowa, N. J.: Rowman
          and Allanhead.

Ruether, Rosemary Radford
  1983a   *Sexism and God-Talk: Toward a Feminist Theology*. Boston:
          Beacon Press.
  1983b   *Women-Church: Theology and Practice*. San Francisco: Harper
          and Row.
  1985   *Womanguides: Readings Toward a Feminist Theology*. Boston:
          Beacon Press.
  1989a   "The Western Religious Tradition and Violence Against
          Women in the Home." In *Christianity, Patriarchy, and Abuse:
          A Feminist Critique*, 31–41. Edited by Joanne Carlson Brown
          and Carole R. Bohn. Cleveland: Pilgrim Press.
  1989b   "The Women Church Movement In Contemporary
          Christianity." In *Women's Leadership in Marginal Religions:
          Explorations Outside the Mainstream*, 169-210. Edited by
          Catherine Wessinger. Urbana, Ill.: University of Illinois
          Press.

Scanzoni, Letha, and Nancy Hardesty
  1974   *All We're Meant to Be: A Biblical Approach to Women's
          Liberation*. Waco, Tex.: Word Books.

Schmalzbauer, John
  1993   "Evangelicals in the New Class: Class Versus Subcultural
          Predictors of Ideology." *Journal for the Scientific Study of
          Religion* 32 (4): 330–42.

Schüssler Fiorenza, Elisabeth
  1985   *In Memory of Her: A Feminist Theological Reconstruction of
          Christian Origins*. New York: Crossroad.
  1992   *But She Said: Feminist Practices of Biblical Interpretation*.
          Boston: Beacon Press.
  1994   "Introduction." In *Concilium: Violence Against Women*,
          i–xxiv. Edited by Elisabeth Schüssler Fiorenza and Mary
          Shawn Copeland. London: SCM Press.

Scott, Joan W.
  1990   "Deconstructing Equality-Versus-Difference: Or, the Uses
          of Poststructuralist Theory of Feminism." In *Conflicts in
          Feminism*, 134–48. Edited by Marianne Hirsch and Evelyn
          Fox Keller. New York: Routledge.

Searl, Natalie
  1994   "The Women's Bible Study: A Thriving Evangelical
          Support Group." In *"I Come Away Stronger": How Small
          Groups are Shaping American Religion*, 97–124. Edited by
          Robert Wuthnow. Grand Rapids, Mich.: Eerdmans.

Sered, Susan Starr
  1994   *Priestess, Mother, Sacred Sister: Religions Dominated by
          Women.* New York: Oxford University Press.

Shibley, Mark A.
  1996   *Resurgent Evangelicalism in the United States: Mapping
          Cultural Change since 1970.* Columbia, S.C.: University of
          South Carolina Press.

Shriver, Peggy L.
  1989   "The Religious Right: A Program of Intolerance and
          Coercion." In *The Religious Right*, 26–30. Edited by Gary E.
          McCuen. Hudson, Wisconsin: Gary McCuen Publications.

Smart, Carol
  1990   "Law's Power, the Sexed Body and Feminist Discourse."
          Journal of Law and Society 17: 194–210.

Smith, Dorothy
  1987   *The Everyday World as Problematic: A Feminist Sociology.*
          Toronto: University of Toronto Press.

Spelman, Elizabeth V.
  1992   "Gender in the Context of Race and Class: Notes on
          Chodorow's 'Reproduction of Mothering.'" In *Feminist
          Philosophies: Problems, Theories, and Applications*, 322–30.
          Edited by Janet A. Kourany, James P. Sterba, and
          Rosemarie Tong. Englewood Cliffs, N.J.: Prentice Hall.

Spencer, A. B.
  1985   *Beyond the Curse: Women Called to Ministry.* Nashville:
          Thomas Nelson.

Stacey, Judith
  1990   *Brave New Families: Stories of Domestic Upheaval in Late
          Twentieth Century America.* New York: Basic Books.

Stacey, Judith, and Susan Elizabeth Gerard
  1990   "'We Are Not Doormats': The Influence of Feminism on
          Contemporary Evangelicals in the United States." In
          Uncertain Terms: Negotiating Gender in American Culture,
          98–117. Edited by Faye Ginsburg. Boston: Beacon Press.

Stacey, William, and Anson Shupe
  1983   *The Family Secret: Domestic Violence in America.* Boston: Beacon Press.

Stackhouse, John G., Jr.
  1993   *Canadian Evangelicalism in the Twentieth Century: An Introduction to Its Character.* Toronto: University of Toronto Press.

Strom, Kay Marshall
  1986   *In the Name of Submission.* Portland, Oreg.: Multnomah Press.

Torjesen, Karen Jo
  1995   *When Women Were Priests: Women's Leadership in the Early Church and the Scandal of their Subordination in the Rise of Christianity.* San Francisco: Harper.

Trebbi, Diana
  1993   "Women-Church: Catholic Women Produce an Alternative Spirituality." In *In Gods We Trust: New Patterns of Religious Pluralism in America,* 347–51. Edited by Thomas Robbins and Dick Anthony. New Brunswick, N.J.: Transaction Publishers.

Wagner, Melinda Bollar
  1990   *God's Schools: Choice and Compromise in American Society.* New Brunswick, N.J.: Rutgers University Press.

Wallace, Cecelia
  1976   "Changes in the Churches." In *Women in the Canadian Mosaic,* 93–128. Edited by Gwen Matheson. Toronto: Peter Martin Associates Limited.

Wallace, Ruth
  1992   *They Call Her Pastor.* Albany, N.Y.: SUNY Press.

Warner, R. Stephen
  1988   *New Wine in Old Wineskins: Evangelicals and Liberals in a Small-Town Church.* Berkeley, Calif.: University of California Press.

Wheeler, Barbara
  1996   "You Who Were Afar Off: Religious Divisions and the Role of Religious Research." *Review of Religious Research* 37 (4): 289–301.

Whipple, Vicky
  1987   "Counseling Battered Women from Fundamentalist Churches." *Journal for Marital and Family Therapy* 13: 385–408.

Wilcox, Clyde
  1994   "Premillenialists at the Millennium: Some Reflections on
          the Christian Right in the Twenty-first Century." *Sociology
          of Religion* 55 (3): 243–61.

Williamson, John B., David A. Karp, John R. Dalphin, and Paul S. Gray
  1982   *The Research Craft: An Introduction to Social Research
          Methods*. Boston: Little, Brown.

Wilson, John, and Marc Musick
  1995   "Personal Autonomy and Religion and Marriage: Is There
          a Link?" *Review of Religious Research* 37 (1): 3–18.

Winston, Diane
  1994   "Answered Prayers: The Rockhaven House Fellowship."
          In *"I Come Away Stronger": How Small Groups are Shaping
          American Religion*, 7–36. Edited by Robert Wuthnow. Grand
          Rapids, Mich.: Eerdmans.

Winter, Miriam Therese, Adair Lummis, and Allison Stokes
  1994   *Defecting in Place: Women Claiming Responsibility for their
          own Spiritual Lives*. New York: Crossroad.

Young, Pamela Dickey
  1992   "Diversity in Feminist Christology." *Studies in Religion*
          21 (1): 81–90.